Bringing in the
SHEAVES ™

Edited by Ken and Janice Tate

HOUSE of
WHITE
BIRCHES

PUBLISHERS
SINCE 1947

Bringing in the Sheaves

Editors: Ken and Janice Tate
Associate Editor: Barb Sprunger
Copy Editors: Läna Schurb, Mary Nowak

Production Coordinator: Brenda Gallmeyer
Design/Production Artist: Beverly Jenkins
Cover Design: Vicki Macy
Traffic Coordinator: Sandra Beres
Production Assistants: Shirley Blalock, Carol Dailey, Marj Morgan, Chad Tate
Photography: Tammy Christian, Jeff Chilcote, Jennifer Fourman
Photography Assistant: Linda Quinlan
Photography Stylist: Arlou Wittwer

Publishers: Carl H. Muselman, Arthur K. Muselman
Chief Executive Officer: John Robinson
Marketing Director: Scott Moss
Product Development Director: Vivian Rothe
Publishing Services Manager: Brenda Wendling

Customer Service: (800) 829-5865
Printed in the United States of America
First Printing: 2000
Library of Congress Number: 99-95551
ISBN: 1-882138-56-2

We would like to thank the following for the art prints used in this book:
Mill Pond Press: "Small Town Church" by Luke Buck, page 19; "Christmas Service" by Jess Hager, pages 42 and 43; "The Insiders" by Don Spaulding, page 160. All by arrangement with Mill Pond Press Inc. For information on art prints, contact Mill Pond Press, Venice, FL 34292, (800) 535-0331.
Wild Wings Inc.: "Harvest Time" by Sam Timm, cover; "Country Charm-Chickadee" by Sam Timm, page 8; "Country Ride" by Persis Clayton Weirs, page 50; "Sunday Morning" by Sam Timm, pages 68 and 69; "Sunday Surprise" by Persis Clayton Weirs, pages 114 and 115; "After the Rain" by Sam Timm, page 85; and "Christmas Village" by Persis Clayton Weirs, page 149. All by arrangement with Wild Wings Inc., Lake City, MN 55041, (800) 445-4833.
We would also like to give a very special thank-you to the First Mennonite Church Historical Society, Berne, Ind., for the use of their photographs on pages 1, 4, 5, 15, 89, 90, 95, 109 and 144, Berne Public Library for the use of their photographs on pages 5, 99, 105, 119, 121 and 146; Henry Ford Museum and Greenfield Village, page 159; Swiss Heritage Village, Berne, Ind., pages 37 and 49; and Danny C. Blevins, page 35.
Photographs on pages 9, 10, 12, 46 and 56 by Janice Tate. Photographs on pages 101 and 129 courtesy Ken and Janice Tate. Hymns in this book are from The Service Hymnal of the Zanesville (Ind.) Church of God, printed in 1964.

Dear Friends of the Good Old Days,

Bringing in the Sheaves! Bringing in the Sheaves! We shall come rejoicing, Bringing in the Sheaves! The words of the old gospel hymn still echo in my mind after all these years. I think I know why. Back in the Good Old Days, church, religion and all things spiritual weren't just things we did once a week—they were a part of our lives. Whether you lived on the farm, in small village or a big city, you knew who God was and what He had done for you, your family, your community and your nation. How many countless prayers had He heard from us about drought, depression and war? And He delivered us collectively from them all.

Being a farm boy, I especially knew what sheaves were. We brought them in every harvest. And I knew early on what Jesus meant when He said, "The harvest truly is great, but the labourers are few ..." (Luke 10:2). Sometimes I wondered if I was the only "labourer" out there. That was never the case; it just felt that way.

Then I came to understand that the sheaves and the harvest were just an analogy about people—family and neighbors, school chums and town folks. That's when I learned what all the rejoicing was about, and I began to see God in almost everything around me.

He was in neighbor helping neighbor after a devastating fire. He was in pie suppers and cake walks to benefit our little country school. He was in yuletide festivals when some magnanimous Santa brought oranges, apples, nuts and maybe even a small toy to us kids who otherwise might not have much of a Christmas.

He was in church, yes—but so much more. He was in births, baptizings, wedded bliss and bereavement. He was on city streets, in country stores, down country lanes to simple homes and, yes, even out in the fields helping a 12-year-old country kid bring in the sheaves.

When my wife, Janice, and I envisioned this book we wanted to bring you the spirit of those Good Old Days. We hope this collection of stories will remind you of the tears, fears, joy and laughter that were the heart and soul of some of that old-time religion. Let your foot and your heart pick up the beat of the old gospel hymn as we again come rejoicing, Bringing in the Sheaves.

Ken Tate

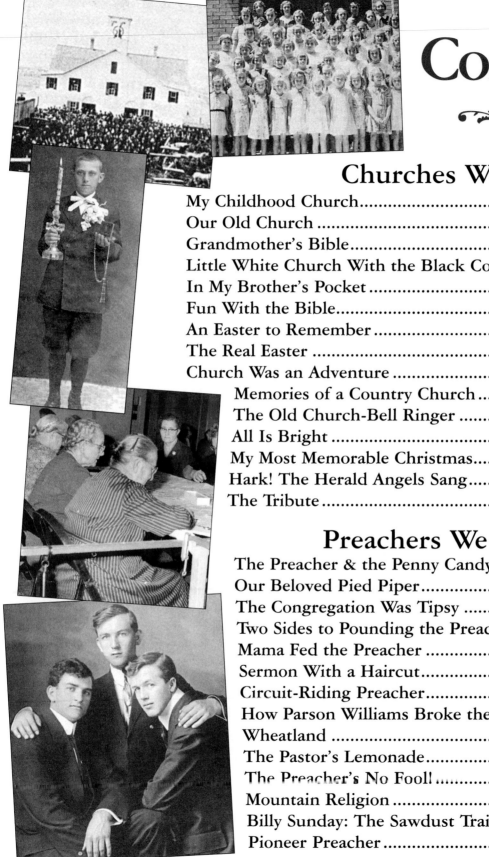

Contents

Churches We Knew • 7

Preachers We Knew • 51

Revivals, Socials & Goin' to Meetin' • 83

Saints, Sinners & Samaritans • 135

John Slobodnik

Churches We Knew

One of my favorite games when I was a child was to imagine buildings and homes were people. An old, abandoned home to me was like a lonely old widow, wishing for company to creak the boards of her front porch again. The blacksmith shop was gruff and masculine, while the millinery was as soft and feminine as bolts of cloths.

Walking down the streets of the nearest Ozark Mountain village to my childhood home, I imagined the barber shop to be warm and friendly as a hot towel on a bearded face—as warm and friendly as barbers Burl and Chick could make it. The factory was big and strong—and maybe just a little scary. In the youthful playground of my mind each edifice had its own peculiarity and personality.

Then there were the churches! In childish innocence I never understood denominations and sects. I just saw people trying to seek God—a noble endeavor, no matter what the name. So, the churches I knew from those Good Old Days became sides to the personality of God Himself.

First there was the Cedar Valley Pentecostal church where my family attended. It showed the exuberance and vitality of the Creator that I saw throughout His creation. A Pentecostal meeting or revival was a lot like following King David, dancing through the streets of Jerusalem, bringing the Ark of the Covenant back to the temple. It was gospel music, "amen" shouting and foot stomping. It—like the Father in Heaven—was so alive.

The Presbyterian Church had the biggest choir, and that choir sounded like a heavenly troupe of angels when it provided special performances around Christmastime. I could imagine the throne of God, surrounded by the most beautiful chorus singing "Hallelujahs" and "Hosannas" to their hearts content. The memories of that choir fill my mind's ears with a melody that remains so vivid today.

Other churches also reflected the ways of God to my young eyes. The First Baptist Church was as solid as a rock; its simple, strong architecture made this youngster believe that it, like God, would always be there. The Presbyterian church with its chiming bell tower reminded me also of His timeless faithfulness. The Catholic Church, with its ornate façade and stained glass, displayed the grandeur and majesty of the Almighty.

Mama and Daddy may not have taken us to services at all the churches in the area, but be they Lutheran, Church of Christ or Assembly of God, I knew them nonetheless. And from them all I came to know my Maker.

In those days of innocence I didn't know about differences in skin color, social status or spirituality. That is one quality we would all like to retain, imperfectly though it might be. But if we have held onto any part of the ideal I believe we owe much of that to our friends—the churches we knew from the Good Old Days.

—Ken Tate

My Childhood Church

By Mr. Shirley A. McCahan

One of the advantages of growing older is that we become richer in memories of our earlier experiences. Many may have been of a disciplinary nature that proved to be an asset in our growth. Not to be overlooked are memories of our church experiences.

I have lived in other areas for many years, but I still feel a strong loyalty to my old home church. This makes my memories sweeter and more sentimental. A few times in recent years, I have made a short weekday visit to the adjacent cemetery and also visited the church for meditation and relaxation, to view the changes in the interior, admire its beauty and enjoy its quiet atmosphere.

In earlier days, many people walked to church. The ringing church bell also intoned to them the Master's invitation to come.

During these visits, as I approached the church, I thought of William Pitts and how he was inspired to write *The Church in the Wildwood*. More than a century ago, his first view of "the little brown church" was from a stagecoach, and he had a longer time to view the exterior and surroundings as he approached. Traveling in an automobile, I approached St. Stephens more quickly, and my thoughts and memories occurred at a rapid rate:

There's a church in Licking Creek Valley,
The quietest place in the locality;
Memories are dearer as I older grow,
Each visit there enriches my soul.

The stained-glass windows and the bell,
Pews, altar, organ have a story to tell,
A story of salvation that's abundant and free
For everyone, yes, for sinners like you and me.

I have many memories of this church in which I was baptized and later confirmed. Once I visited and worshiped at a Sunday-morning service, my first at St. Stephens in more than 36 years. Only three things had remained unchanged: the stained-glass windows, the bell and the minister.

Those cathedral-style windows have remained beautiful. Just as the sunlight strengthens, beautifies and penetrates the plants of the earth and the atmosphere, so the stained-glass windows allow the sun's rays to penetrate the atmosphere within. We are reminded of the light of Christ, our Savior, beautifying our lives and penetrating our lives in His service.

The loved one in whose name those windows were given reminds us of our predecessors who worshiped there before us, who gave us our Christian heritage. They were concerned for those who came later, and expressed their love by a Christian witness of their faith in a living, omnipotent God.

The stained-glass windows also tell of the donor's thoughtfulness and appreciation for his Christian legacy made possible by an older generation, and they indicate the donor's continued benevolence.

The second unchanged thing is the bell. There was a time when not every person had a watch (before the invention of wristwatches); and, if the only clock in the home was incorrect, the ringing of the first bell reminded people it was time to leave for church. Many people set their clock by the church bell (there was no television or radio in those days).

In earlier days, many people walked to church. The ringing church bell also intoned to them the Master's invitation to come—more specifically, "Come unto Me"—plus all the promises related to His invitation. To many people, its ringing gave a sentimental reminder of one gone before. To some, it's an inspiration of the present; to others, a vision of the future; to others, the ringing of the bell is music to their soul.

As for the minister, I cannot find words to express my appreciation and thankfulness for his help and services over the years. He is still a

living example of helpfulness and all other virtues. He has been our eyes for everything good. Surely the Spirit of God dwells richly in him.

But my thoughts and recollections travel over a span of years beyond those 36. Many years ago, when we lived only two miles from the church, we tried to be ready at least a half-hour before time for the afternoon services. In winter, we had to curry, harness and hitch the horse to the buggy or carriage (or sleigh or sled if we had snow), and also fill the firebox in the kitchen range with wood so it would be warm when we returned. On reaching the church, we tied and blanketed the horse.

There were no shortcuts in worship; it was often lengthy. When Father was on the council, that extra half-hour after church seemed unnecessary to a 5- to 7-year-old boy, but as I became older, I soon realized the importance and responsibilities of the council. Now, with the turn of the key and fast, convenient transportation, many people are less loyal to their church and complain about the effort.

In summertime, we used fly nets on the horse. Some greased the insides of their horse's ears to reduce fly bites. As soon as weather permitted each spring, it was the son's assignment to wash the buggy or carriage and make sure all spring mud was removed. Son was rewarded with a nickel for a job well done—honorable pay for a boy in those days.

Among my memories are a row of hitching posts and several large trees bearing tie rings. The large trees became unsafe for tying, especially when stormy, so our fathers had a frolic fund-raiser to build a tying shed. Many families gave lumber. Many members gave free labor and time. As a result, a shed was built long enough to accommodate 14 rigs and their horses. The first stall was reserved for the minister, and the second for the Sunday school superintendent. The shed served its purpose for many years, but with the advent of automobiles, the shed soon became unused and deteriorated, and it was finally removed.

Only three things had remained unchanged at St. Stephens in more than 36 years: the stained-glass windows, the bell and the minister.

On my visit to my childhood church, I found a modern, paved, well-marked parking lot with space for 30–40 parked cars. The hitching posts and trees have been gone for many years. The space between the parking lot and the creek is covered with high grass and tall weeds. The creek is no long visible. Those many years ago it was a common cow pasture for a few non-farming residents. During the week, the cows kept the grass short. On Sundays it served as a hitching area, and the creek added serenity and beauty to the setting.

Early in the century, industrial progress was slow, but our spiritual growth was part of our daily living. All ladies wore hats in church and their ankles were not seen. Most girls wore hair ribbons. Many plaited their hair. Most people wore button shoes; a shoe hook was a necessity. Boys wore knee pants until they were 16 years old. I was promised a pair of long pants when I joined the church.

Many girls had a long dress made for the occasion of joining the church. But that long dress served another purpose, too: It let everyone know she was old enough to have a beau (we didn't call him a "boyfriend" in those days). Some girls, at this epoch in their lives, also started a hope chest—an asset for any marriageable girl (there were no credit cards back then, either).

Among other things are memories of church funerals. That was before the days of funeral parlors; "mortician" and "funeral director" were unknown terms in those days. They were known as "undertakers," and they usually ran a furniture store to supplement their income. Time and progress soon added dignity to the profession and a more attractive title. I remember the horse-drawn hearse—black for an adult, white for a child. The pallbearers (carriers) wore gloves (furnished by the undertaker) to match the hearse.

My father was a member of a quartet that sang regularly at funerals. One song they sang was *There Will Be No Dark Valley When Jesus*

Comes. A public viewing usually followed a lengthy service. In spring, when mud was deep, four horses were often used. The driver sat outside in front. The immediate family wore black. It was a necessity for every adult lady to have a black dress and accessories to wear on such occasions. Men wore black ties, black hats and dark suits.

Another memorable occasion was the annual Harvest Home Service, when the church was decorated with products from the farm—fresh fruit, home-canned food, dried foods and grain from the field. Often the preacher received those products that the members had donated and displayed in the front of the church near the chancel railing. Some considered it part of the preacher's low salary. During the summer, it was common practice for a farmer to deliver a load of hay to the parsonage barn to feed the minister's horse which he was required to own and maintain in those days. Most ministers had more than one church in their parish.

When I was a lad, the minister and his family were invited to our home for a meal. At their departure, Mother always gave them eggs, country butter, a chicken or a slice of home-cured ham. Father would put a bag of oats in the buggy box. I know it's hard for young folks nowadays to comprehend what might be called "forgotten generosity," but it was a way of life. It was an expression of love, unselfishly offered.

I cannot forget the Christmas programs, when each child received a small box of candy and a large orange. Think of all the time and effort and joys associated with it. Let us not forget the annual Children's Day program and the annual Sunday-school picnic—not in an amusement park, but in a quiet location with a home-cooked dinner and a program in which we all took part. And who could forget the wintertime revivals?

One could write at length about the different members who attended my childhood church—the tobacco-chewing deacon who always carried his tobacco to church, the eccentric old man, the woman with the largest hat—and the behavior of children, including my own, which was controlled by strict parental discipline.

In early days, worshipers lingered after the services in neighborly fellowship and exchanged news, and inquired about the welfare of others.

In early days, worshipers lingered after the services in neighborly fellowship and exchanged news, and inquired about the welfare of others. (The telephone was just making its debut; only the prosperous enjoyed a daily newspaper, and it arrived a day late.) Today everyone is in a hurry to get home so they can go on a picnic, watch a ball game or play golf.

Just as animals thirst for water at the end of the race, so thirsts my soul for communion with God and the fellowship of friends. And I owe it to the church of my childhood. ❖

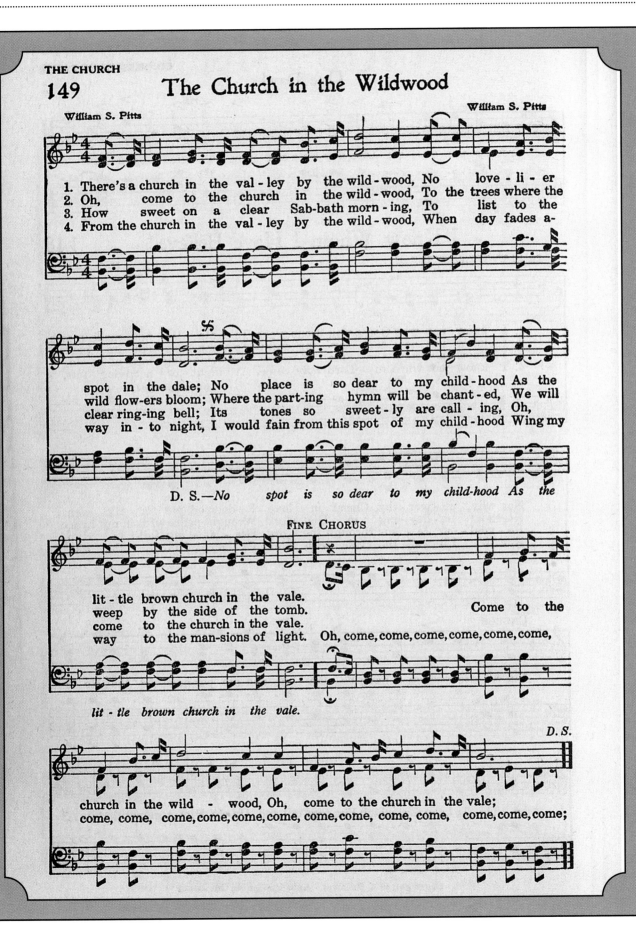

THE CHURCH

149 The Church in the Wildwood

William S. Pitts

William S. Pitts

1. There's a church in the val-ley by the wild-wood, No love-li-er
2. Oh, come to the church in the wild-wood, To the trees where the
3. How sweet on a clear Sab-bath morn-ing, To list to the
4. From the church in the val-ley by the wild-wood, When day fades a-

spot in the dale; No place is so dear to my child-hood As the
wild flow-ers bloom; Where the part-ing hymn will be chant-ed, We will
clear ring-ing bell; Its tones so sweet-ly are call-ing, Oh,
way in-to night, I would fain from this spot of my child-hood Wing my

D. S.—No spot is so dear to my child-hood As the

FINE CHORUS

lit-tle brown church in the vale.
weep by the side of the tomb.
come to the church in the vale.
way to the man-sions of light. Oh, come, come, come, come, come, come,

Come to the

lit-tle brown church in the vale.

D. S.

church in the wild-wood, Oh, come to the church in the vale;
come, come, come, come, come, come, come, come, come, come, come, come, come;

Our Old Church

By Marguerite Getz

During the early years of this century, I was a child living with my parents and sisters on a farm in southwestern Ohio. It was near the little village of Jacksonburg, which has long been nationally famous for two reasons. It happens to be the smallest incorporated town in the state of Ohio, and it is also the birthplace of James M. Cox who was governor of Ohio during 1913–1915. In 1920, he ran for president of the United States on the Democratic ticket with Franklin D. Roosevelt as his running mate. All of us kids around Jacksonburg were really keyed up over that election, but we had a big letdown when Warren G. Harding defeated him.

Mr. Cox was a good friend of my father's, and he often visited in our home. We considered him our good neighbor, as our farm joined the one he owned. He had made a showplace of his old homestead. It is still beautiful today.

He served as a part-time janitor at the old church he attended as a boy. He often said how proud he was on Sunday mornings to ring the old bell that called the people to worship.

Years later, this was the church I attended in my youth, along with my family. There were very few cars at that time and, like the other people, we rode there in our buggy or surrey. We tied our horse to a hitching post at the side of the building. In winter, we were always glad to get there and get inside where the place was heated by two potbellied stoves. They had to be stoked and replenished often during the service.

There were very few cars at that time and we rode there in our buggy or surrey. We tied our horse to a hitching post at the side of the building.

I still remember the old fellow who had this job and the racket he made as he poked the coals and rattled that old coal bucket. It always seemed to happen at prayer time. We children couldn't hold back the giggles, and that meant a scolding on the way home.

The church was lit with kerosene lamps, as our homes were. Then, one year, it was decided to install an acetylene light plant. A huge tank of carbide was put in the basement to supply the fuel for the big chandelier in the center of the room and for the lights in brackets along the walls.

My father was not in favor of this new system as he thought so many open flames in the fixtures were too dangerous. If one or more were to be blown out by a breeze, the room would fill with fumes.

So Dad was very reluctant to take us to any night services. But one

evening we did coax him to go. Right in the middle of the sermon, every light went out, and the room was in total darkness. The preacher immediately requested that everyone remain seated and asked that no one light a match. Someone was to go to the basement to locate the trouble. Right then my father told Mom and us kids to get ready to leave.

Holding hands and led by Dad, we stumbled over people's feet on our way to the door and then out to the middle of the street. He kept grumbling all the way, "I'm not listening to that preacher and running a chance of being blown to smithereens!"

We waited for a few minutes and soon the lights came back on. The preacher went on with his sermon, but my dad was either too scared or too embarrassed to go back in. He unhitched old Pet and we all got in our surrey and headed for home.

A few years later, when I was a teenager, a new stone church was built. James Cox contributed a large sum of money and his architect drew up the plans.

All the farmers hauled stones from a creek nearby. When the beautiful church was completed, there was a big day of dedication and celebration. Mr. Cox was the main speaker. He told again about his boyhood days of training in the old building and how he loved ringing the bell on Sunday mornings.

That same old bell was hung in the new church, and it still rings every Sunday, calling the people of that community to worship. ❖

Grandmother's Bible

By Lillian P. McGee

Remember the days of Grandmother and her Good Book?

Well, I finally went back to church—Mount Beaser Primitive Baptist in Sopchoppy, Fla.,—a small rural church with whitewashed stuccoed walls and a homemade steeple with an even smaller congregation.

A friend and fellow employee and his wife had invited me, along with my two small children, on this particular Sunday.

As in many churches, everyone totes his or her own Bible so they can read along with the preacher when he cites certain scriptures.

I was embarrassed when, after entering this sanctuary, I found I had neglected to bring a Bible.

My friend, being most perceptive to the feelings of others, immediately noticed that I was the only one without the "Good Book," as they call it in Sopchoppy.

Without hesitation, Frances, my friend's wife, was kind enough to place her Bible in my hands. She said she could share her husband's Bible during the service.

When she placed the book in my hands, I immediately knew that this was not just any Bible. It was soft and worn from dutiful use, torn and tattered, and yet it still gleamed radiantly in the stained-glass light of the church window, as would any jewel.

As I opened its covers, I noticed that many words and phrases had been underlined, and I felt love. That's the only word I can use to describe what was contained in this treasured book—not just the content, but the way it was used and the way it shaped someone's life; someone who not only read this book, but who lived this book.

With fond and nostalgic feelings, I began to remember ever so vividly that my grandmother's Bible was a huge part of her.

Her Bible had great significance to me. When I rambled around her big, old, "scary," antebellum house every night of the summers I spent with her, the last thing I would see before bedtime was grandmother reading her Bible in bed with the assistance of a dim lamp. In her expression and her eyes, I could see an indescribable reverence.

Every night this sight would comfort me so much that I could securely go to sleep in her big, old, scary, house.

Sometimes I would creep into Grandmother's room during the day and, ever so gently, remove her Bible from the drawer of her little bedside stand.

I would thumb through the pages and always see where she had kept her place from the night before and—like Frances—had underlined passages that were important to her life.

Also, I would always look at my childhood picture that she kept tucked away within the pages. It made me feel special because mine was the only picture she kept in this treasured book. It was always there, along with a $100 bill she kept for my mother to have when, one day, Grandmother passed away.

All these warm thoughts consumed me during the church service I attended that day, and when it ended, my eyes were wet with tears as the memories came flooding back.

I cannot honestly tell you what the good preacher said that day, but I can say that I felt in some way that I had come home again.

I don't know what happened to my grandmother's Bible after her departure from this world, but I do know that she would have wanted me to have it. I always knew that.

I would give every material thing I own to have that Bible. However, even though I don't, I rediscovered a very important part of myself: that my grandmother and her "Good Book" will always have a vivid place in my soul. ❖

A.M.E.'s Super Suppers

By Francis Xavier Sculley

With a voice that would shatter glass, the short, barrel-chested, coal-black man exhorted his flock to follow the path of righteousness. Pausing for effect, he looked over the top of his glasses that were as thick as the plate glass in the front door of the little church. Raising his hands in supplication, he prayed for the deliverance of his flock.

Was there ever such a man as the Rev. Cuff? People three blocks away heard his sermons, without ever leaving the comfort of their front porch, and when he led the congregation in song, people passing on the street stopped to listen to the deepest bass they had ever heard.

Often, coming home from Mass on a Sunday morning, I would stop to watch the powerful man shake hands with his faithful little band, which never numbered more than 30. The Rev. Cuff never failed to wave across the street to his little white friends on their way home from their own church, nor did he ever fail to reach down and pat the head of every little black girl and boy in attendance.

Known as the African Methodist Episcopal Church of Zion, the little house of worship was built on the corner of Bank and Mechanic streets, right in the heart of the residential district of Bradford, Pa. The tiny church was less than a block from some of the wealthiest families in Pennsylvania's lush oil region. Dedicated one beautiful day back in 1922, the pretty little church was the pride and joy of the eight or 10 black families living in the high-grade oil metropolis.

But the one thing that will be remembered

Remembering the little white church with the black congregation.

more than anything else about the A.M.E. Church would be its wonderful, weekly suppers held in the spotless basement.

On a Monday evening, long tables with white tablecloths and gleaming tableware would be readied for the diners who surged through the doors beginning at 4 o'clock. The tables soon filled, while dozens either stood outside or leaned against the wall awaiting their turn.

"My, how that boy do grow! I remember when his mama was pushing him in that big, gray buggy. Now how about some corn fritters, son?" asked Mrs. Logan as she greeted my uncle and me one evening.

Never had I seen such a stack of chicken and biscuits; rubber-legged after two helpings plus at least a dozen corn fritters, I could hardly move.

"Now you just sit right down here. We have pecan pie with whipped cream or hot mince pie. And you better have another glass of milk, if you expect to be a soldier like your daddy was," admonished the wonderful old lady.

When it was all over, I practically had to be led to the door. The Rev. Cuff shouted after us, "We're having baked ham and candied sweets next week, and more of them rolls. Y'all be sure and come, won't you?"

The little church still stands as it did years ago, and spirituals still float out across the valley. But the voices of the Rev. Cuff, Mrs. Allen and Mrs. Logan must now be heard in a heavenly choir.

The church suppers are now a thing of the past, too. But sometimes it seems as if I can almost hear the rattle of the tableware and smell the delicious aroma of Mrs. Allen's pecan pie. ❖

In My Brother's Pocket

By Katherine Von Ahnen

I remember with pleasure many houses that I lived in as a child in the little seaside town of Cape May, N.J. Each had its own personality, from the little whitewashed house on Pearl Avenue to the big duplex on Broadway. Wicker and rattan furniture, iron bedsteads, a long cupboard-lined pantry where hot pies or freshly baked cakes were set to cool, winding, circular stairways, and little odd-shaped stained-glass windows—all were part of a happy childhood, lovingly remembered. Once I had a bedroom closet that was so large, I also kept my writing desk in it.

Some of my childhood homes had big back yards with swings in huge leafy trees, and some had front "lawns" with hedges and flowers. There were screened-in front porches and back sheds where the laundry was done. I don't remember any basements, but I do remember the attics!

Attics were big expanses where out-of-season things were stored, like clothing that hung from the rafters in mothball scented garment bags, huge comforters and feather beds, suitcases, big cardboard boxes full of interesting items, trunks, flower seeds in colorful mesh bags, and toys that my brother and I had outgrown. Attics somehow had a mystical air about them that made me feel as if I had left the real world behind and entered into a wondrous world of fantasy, especially on a rainy day.

What was the one house that gave me the values and principles that have sustained me all my life? It was the House of God.

All of the houses of my childhood were important to me, and yet, not one more than the other. Where then, is the one house that gave me the values and principles that have sustained me all my life? The answer is so simple. It was the House of God.

The first house that had a lasting effect upon my life was the Union Chapel at Broadway and Sixth Avenue in Cape May. It was a square, white, frame building with a simple bell tower. The sound of that bell pealing every Sunday afternoon at 2 o'clock still rings deep and true in my memory.

Union Chapel sat proudly on a green, grassy corner lot. Cement walkways led to two whitewashed outhouses. The square stained-glass windows looked out upon the passersby and entreated all to enter. Inside there was a large main room, with many wooden benches and a small stage or pulpit.

Directly behind the stage was the "primary" room. I remember the Cradle Roll that was prominently displayed on the wall. It had little gold cradles suspended on blue and pink satin ribbons. Each cradle bore the name of a newborn.

We had long plank tables for coloring or drawing, and square, wooden boxes to sit on. They were painted bright green. There was a big brown piano and from its keys tinkled *Jesus Loves Me, Jesus Loves the Little Children of the World* and seasonal songs like *Jingle Bells* and *The First Easter Morning.*

Mrs. Reeves was my primary teacher. She also doubled as pianist. She wore her blond hair in waves set close to her head. Her hands always seemed to be flying around, like birds. She wore a lot of flowered dresses with lace collars, and she smelled just like lilacs. I thought she was the smartest lady in the world, and I believed everything she taught us with an absolute and all-encompassing faith.

After our little songs and prayers, we had our Bible lesson. Some of them frightened me and some of them delighted me, but all of them held me in complete awe. Each child had a two-page leaflet with a picture we could color on the outside, and a Bible story on the inside. We were always encouraged to choose the closing song. It was invariably *Jesus Loves Me* and we could really belt it out.

As our voices ascended heavenward, I'm sure God stopped whatever He was doing, so He could really enjoy the sound of the children of the Union Chapel Primary as they worshiped Him at the top of their lungs.

When I was 7 or 8 years old, I graduated from the primary department to the "big room." It was exciting and frightening. For many years I had heard loud and important sounds coming from that room, and now I was going to be a part of it. There was a graduation ceremony on the stage. I wore a brand-new white dress with ruffles and a pink sash, pink socks, and white, patent-leather, one-buckle Mary Janes. Several of us stood in a line while the superintendent of the chapel presented us with little gold-and-white pins. Mine was then—as it is now—one of my most prized possessions.

In the "big room" I found myself in a U-shaped cubicle made of big wooden benches. A new teacher, some new friends and a whole new way of learning about God greeted me. The beautiful new adult hymns were like magic to me. I didn't understand all the words, but deep in my heart, I knew they were the right ones.

I was in the fifth grade before I realized the "old rugged cross" was not a big cross on a hill far away where people threw their old rugs because they did not want to suffer the shame of using those old rugs in their houses. I also thought the mystery of the "Our Father" would be revealed to me now that I was in the "big room." But no! Grown-ups went right on addressing God as "Our Father" (which was Okay), but then still followed it up by demanding to know who was in heaven, and then told Him that His name was hollowed. Strange indeed!

I learned many, many Bible verses. My favorite one was "God is love." To me, those three words seemed to have the power to solve every problem in the world. Besides that, it was very short and easy to learn. We received a little card for each Bible verse we learned. When we had 150 cards, we were given a little Bible. I still have mine, and my favorite Bible verse is still "God is love."

When I was in the sixth grade, my family moved to Cape May Court House, a little inland town and the county seat. My brother and I became members of the First Baptist Church. It was a beautiful red-brick building with two towers, and an immense circular stained-glass window. On a sunny Easter morning, my brother and I were baptized in a pool beneath the pulpit. Pastor Haines talked to us long and seriously about our decision to be baptized. It was a plunge in more ways than one. I had always been sure that I was God's child, but now, finally, I was sure that he knew it, too.

After I was baptized, I had the feeling the eye of God was upon me 24 hours a day, walking and sleeping. It was really very scary, but I learned to live with it.

I would write a little verse to use as grace for our Sunday dinners when my grandparents came to visit. Everyone was very pleased and said so, but inside of me, I had this delicious secret with God. He knew, and I knew, that while it was good to please other people (especially grown-ups), I was really writing my little verses for His pleasure.

Gladys Erickson, my Sunday-school teacher, had blue eyes, a beautiful smile, and gold braids wrapped around her head like a crown. Even though she looked like an angel, she was a very down-to-earth person. She showed the same delight and pleasure when she met me unexpectedly on Main Street that she displayed on Sunday mornings at church when I walked into class. She always made me feel as if we shared a very special relationship. It was relationship that I experienced in reverse many years later when I was a Camp Fire leader for a wonder group of young girls. God sure turns the tables sometimes.

If there ever was a perfect Christian woman, it was Vera Sayres. She played the piano for the junior choir. Vera Sayres was brightly colored balls of yarn turning into caps and mittens, chaperone for our teenage parties, a warm hug on a cold day, adult escort for the Christmas carolers, bouquets of backyard flowers and driver for every trip our junior choir made. She never turned anyone away. The only time I ever doubted God's wisdom was when she was killed by an express train while delivering Christmas food and clothing to the needy. I kept telling myself that God had not killed her; He had simply taken her home to live with Him. It was a bitter lesson to learn, but I came to know that faith is truly the evidence of things not seen or understood.

Christmas Eve candlelight service was a real enchantment. With the organ playing softly, the church illuminated only by flickering candles, and the scent of pine heavy in the air, I could almost hear the flutter of angels' wings as silent prayers ascended heavenward. The beauty of that holy service combined with the silence of a deep inner reverence was an everlasting experience. In reality, the candles glimmer on

The beautiful new adult hymns were like magic to me. I didn't understand all the words, but deep in my heart, I knew they were the right ones.

only in my memory, but that deep inner feeling binds me to God eternally.

I always knew God was there, wherever I was. I came to know Him not as a stern-faced God, but as a being who had a great sense of humor. One Easter Sunday morning, we had a sunrise service on the beach at Stone Harbor. The sun rose, but its rays were obscured by a gray pearled fog that touched everything in sight with silver fingers.

While we were singing, I looked around at all the beauty there. The early morning mist hung like sparkling diamonds on the sea grass that topped the graceful white dunes. Shimmering phosphorus rippled on the face of the ocean. Little black and white sandpipers danced with the white lace waves on the clean, crisp sand.

"Well, God," I said confidentially, "You've really outdone yourself this time!"

God laughed and brought out the sun. For just a few seconds the whole world turned to iridescent gold! Never had His handiwork been more breathtaking.

If cleanliness is next to godliness, then surely cleanliness was Wednesday, and godliness was Sunday. Every Wednesday after school, my brother and I attended junior choir practice. It was also the day the church was cleaned. It smelled of wood and wax and lemon oil. The fragrance of flowers and ferns teased my senses. The linen smell of the big Bible and the hymnbooks intermingled with the scent of crayons from the children's room. I hurried to be the first one there. I enjoyed being alone in the church. It was like being alone with God.

Our junior choir must have learned every hymn in the world, and I loved them all. I still knew the words were right. But finally I understood them. I must have heard a million sermons and listened to a million Sunday-school lessons, but it was through the hymns of my childhood that I came to know God as a friend who would always be there and never let me down.

Our choir traveled to many churches in south Jersey. Finding God in a new church was a source of great delight to me. I tried to explain how I felt to my brother.

"You really think God is everywhere?" he said.

"Yes, I sure do!" I retorted.

"Well then," my brother said tauntingly, "do you think He's in my pocket eating my candy bar?"

It became one of our private jokes. Many years later, when my brother was half a world away in the Air Force, I would write to him and say, "I hope God is still in your pocket."

One day, when my brother was flying over New Hebrides, God reversed our little joke, and put my brother in His pocket. Of all the solemn and serious occasions I remember in that house of God's, nothing will ever equal the sight of that flag-draped casket. It was my brother's favorite hymn, *No Night There*, from the days we shared in junior choir, and it softened my razor-edge grief.

"In the land of fadeless day,

Lies a city, four square,

It shall never pass away,

For there is no night there."

Somehow, I knew those words were right, and I understood that my brother was safe, forever.

The days of my childhood have long passed away. The intervening years have known tears and laughter, success and failure, feast and famine, but somewhere in the quiet recess of my soul, my heart remembers every word of every hymn I ever learned in God's house. That memory is my inner strength and my outer faith.

It makes me now, as I was then, a child of God forever, for I spent my childhood in His house, learning for all time that truly, "God is love." ❖

Fun With the Bible

By Sylva Mularchyk

I was just 13 and life was wonderful—so exciting, I couldn't find time for everything I wanted to do. I did go to Sunday school, but it was because my parents insisted. I wasn't really very much interested.

My Sunday-school teacher was an elderly woman, very sweet and patient, but I was sure she had never been a girl my age. I was positive she couldn't understand my interests, my love of sports and games and animals, especially horses and dogs. Her first name was Alice, but of course, we always called her Miss Frazee. She lived with her sister, Anne, a tiny wisp of a woman like herself. Now that I look back, I wonder at their perseverance, their incredible forbearance. Such wonderful Christian women—how could they put up with a hoyden like me?

Miss Frazee gave each member of her class a Bible when lessons were completed and certain Bible verses memorized. I had never received a Bible, but I knew I didn't deserve one.

I tried to pretend indifference, but I really did envy the girls who proudly carried the Bibles Miss Frazee had presented them. But I thought it was too much work, although I did like history, and when people and events were concerned, I paid a little more attention.

The Frazee sisters regularly invited members of their Sunday-school classes to their home on Saturday afternoons. Naturally I was invited too, every week, but naturally, I was too busy to go. I wanted to play baseball with the boys, ride my horse, go swimming in summer, sledding in winter, whatever the gang was doing. I couldn't waste a whole Saturday afternoon!

The other girls told me they really enjoyed those afternoons. "It isn't like Sunday school. It isn't a class," they told me. "It's fun. We are building a city out of paper cutouts. It will be just like Jerusalem, Miss Alice says. And we are cutting out people, too. And we will move them around and have them act out the Bible stories.

And every Saturday, just before it's time to go home, we have cookies and milk."

The cookies and milk didn't make spending an afternoon indoors worthwhile, but I was intrigued with the city they were building. "Is Jerusalem finished yet?" I asked.

"Oh, no. It takes a long time. We want everything to be just right. We really do need help, Sylva. You should come next Saturday."

When Miss Frazee repeated her invitation again and when Saturday afternoon came around again, I thought, Why don't I go—just once? And so I did.

I'd had no idea what intricate work my friends were doing. The city was laid out on a large table—all the little houses and temples and walls and gardens were being cut from heavy paper and fitted together in a three-dimensional way. Each piece was colored and true to scale. The people were cutouts, too, with various changes of clothing. Everything could be moved and rearranged. It was a marvel!

The Bible characters were all there, from the early times of Jerusalem. And, of course, there were Jesus and His mother, His apostles, Mary Magdalene, Lazarus and his sisters—all those who figured in Bible history.

I was fascinated. The stories became real to me—the people became my friends. Though she had never been in Jerusalem, Miss Frazee knew nearly every street, every building of note, and she explained it all to us.

After that, I never missed a Saturday afternoon at the Frazee home. Those dear ladies made the Bible live for me. I found that I could work in all the activities I loved so much and still have room for Bible study, too.

And the day came when I, too, was presented with a Bible by Miss Frazee. I have it yet—and cherish it and remember, with love, the dear lady who gave it to me. ❖

An Easter to Remember

By Verla A. Mooth

Growing up in the Ozarks of southwestern Missouri, we were deprived of many things. One thing that was not lacking, however, was a Christian heritage. Our small community did not have a church in which to worship, but we gathered in the schoolhouse each Sunday for Sunday school and preaching. If there was no preacher, we sang hymns and shared testimonies.

From the time I was a small child, I had been asked to sing in the choir. I often sang solos, and I participated in all the special programs.

Although Easter Sunday was always observed in a special way, the spring of 1933 was something different. A few years earlier, some in the community had attended an Easter sunrise service in a city park 20 miles away. It was often mentioned as being the most inspirational service they had ever attended.

As Easter drew near, someone suggested that we hold our own sunrise service. Grandpa George suggested we could use his cow pasture down the hollow from where we lived. It was a nice, wide hollow with steep hills on each side. The grazing cows had kept the grass and weeds eaten so low it was almost like a mowed lawn. He said he would move the cows to another pasture. Those who had trucks and cars could park them at his house and walk down to the hollow. The service was set for 6 a.m. Everyone was excited about planning our own sunrise service, but no one was more excited than I was. I had been asked to sing the closing song, *Christ Arose.*

Mama always tried to help me have more confidence in myself by telling me that I was just as pretty as my sister was.

Mama had been saving her egg money to buy material to make me a new dress for Easter. Mama always tried to help me have more confidence in myself by telling me that I was just as pretty as my sister was. My sister was four years older than I was and all of my life I had lived in her shadow. She had dark brown hair and lovely hazel eyes and had developed into a young woman at an early age.

I was tall and skinny and had blue eyes and light brown hair. Many times those blue eyes filled with tears when some thoughtless person was overheard comparing me to my sister. "Verla is smart and she can sing and recite as good as anyone, but she is so plain while her sister is so good-looking!"

Mama would comfort me by saying, "Pretty is as pretty does." I assumed she meant that I was "pretty does." The pain of comparison entombed me in a grave of doubting my own self-worth.

Mama had seen a picture of a lovely dress in the catalog. She bought pale yellow voile and cut out a sleeveless dress and a short jacket with several rows of gathered ruffles that made the jacket look like the petals on a flower. It was the most beautiful, grown-up fashion I had ever had. Mama told me how lovely I looked, but I still had grave doubts.

Easter Sunday we awoke to a cold, drizzling rain. The sky was dark and overcast. Mama started to get out the winter coats. Spring coats were a luxury we couldn't afford. When Mama handed me mine, I laid it on a chair and said, "Mama, I will not wear that old, worn-out coat. I want to show my beautiful new dress." Mama tried to convince me that I would freeze and catch my death of cold, but I was determined.

We hadn't walked any distance down the hollow before I was shivering, but I didn't mention it. I walked along with my head down to keep my face warm, oblivious to my surroundings.

We arrived at the place the service was to be held just as friends and neighbors began to gather. It had been decided that the singers would stand on the hillside. Everyone huddled together to keep warm. Although the choir tried to put feeling into their words, our teeth chattered.

We had secured a preacher for the special event. He put deep feeling into his message of the resurrection and spirits began to lift. A few loud "Amens!" could be heard from the crowd.

I forgot about being cold and listened intently. Soon it was time for my solo. Just as I stepped out a few feet from the others and started the first line of my song, "Low in a grave He lay," the clouds parted and a glorious burst of sunlight rose above the hillside, flooding the hollow with warming rays of light. The bright beams of sun hit squarely in my face, casting a radiant glow on my yellow dress.

I felt warm all over! The words of the song, "He arose, He arose," sounded against the other side of the hill and echoed back through the valley below. I suddenly realized that the ground beneath my feet was covered with beautiful spring violets and wood daisies.

The service was over. Comments about how beautiful the sunrise service was and how we should do it again each year could be heard through the crowd.

On the way home, Mama put her arm around me as we walked along and said, "Honey, I was so proud of you. The sun shining upon your face as you sang made you look just like a beautiful spring flower bursting into bloom."

I whispered back in an awed voice, "It is all right, Mama. I think I now understand what Easter is all about." And it was true. Never again would I compare myself with anyone else. I was God's beautiful creation in my own right. As we left the meadowlands and entered a wood, I saw that all of the dogwood, redbud and wild cherry trees were in full bloom, each different but beautiful in its own way.

It was at that moment that the final wrapping of the shroud of self-doubt which had bound me for 14 years was laid aside. On that unforgettable Easter Sunday morning almost 65 years ago, my spirit burst forth in songs of praise, harmonizing with the birds who were singing their own songs of Easter praise to the Creator. ❖

The Real Easter

By Evelyn Schneider

When I was a child, Easter meant Easter eggs and bunnies. Later in life, it meant something new for Easter, like a pretty dress, some black patent-leather slippers or a hat—always a hat. No one went to church without a hat, and more times than not, it was a new hat. Sometimes my mother and sister would hitch up old Molly to a buggy and drive to a small town 10 miles from our home to a millinery shop.

There we would try on lots of hats, or Mother would let the milliner lady trim her hat with a new cluster of flowers and a new ribbon, or even a cluster of bright cherries.

That became a tradition for me as a teenager—wearing something new to church on Easter Sunday morning. Of course, white gloves were needed to complete the outfit.

As I matured, I began to think more seriously about Jesus dying on the cross. But He arose, so Easter brings a new beginning, new hope, new life.

All Easters are special, but one especially comes to mind often. My little grandson was very ill the week of Easter, and we got a call that they were not sure that he would make it. We prayed that it would be God's will that he would become well. Our thoughts

As I matured, I began to think more seriously about Jesus dying on the cross.

and prayers were with him and his parents, many miles from us.

On Easter Sunday, just as we were leaving for church, the telephone rang. It was my family, calling to tell us their little one was recovering. We went to church thankful and rejoicing.

There is a sense of newness and hope during this season when nature awakens to new life. I am reminded of the song *Because He Lives, I Can Face Tomorrow*—all because of Easter. ❖

Church Was an Adventure

By Bruce Kunath

When I was a kid in the '50s, it was a major task to get ready for church on Sunday.

My brother and I were expected to do homework for Sunday school, but often we only began to study on Saturday evenings, when we were more interested in watching The Jackie Gleason Show on television. We also had to polish our shoes, which was a dirty job.

We had rags, brushes, and cans of black and brown polishes like bootblacks carried. And we were expected to wash our hair, which was no fun either, because we used regular bath soap, which doesn't feel good in one's eye.

When Sunday morning came, my father cooked a delicious breakfast with scrambled eggs for everyone—something we didn't usually have time for during the week.

One time after the service was over, I waited by our '54 Plymouth for my parents and began throwing snowballs at passing cars.

Getting dressed for church was an ordeal. We wore suit jackets with scratchy wool pants, dress shirts with fancy cuff links, and ties that I always felt were choking me. We went through a stage where we experimented with bow ties and Western bolo ties.

We were quite proud of some of our outfits, which were actually tacky looking. I had one outfit that included a green corduroy jacket, pink shirt and a hideous wide tie that was pink and black and had pleats in it. We folded colorful silk handkerchiefs into triangles and stuck them in our suit breast pockets.

My father wore old-fashioned three-piece suits with pinstripes. He rode to work every day with other men who smoked and every night he had to hang his suits outside to try to get rid of the odor. He also had some fancy, large, aftershave bottles; they looked like liquor bottles to me, but he sure smelled good on Sundays.

My brother and I slicked our hair down with Brylcreem. My mother complained that the part I made in my hair was "as crooked as a dog's hind leg." When we got into junior high school, we switched to crew cuts, which we kept bristled with a wax.

Our mother put on her Sunday best, including a hat with a veil, while my father nervously paced the floor, waiting for her. She also had a mink stole, which was highly prized by women in those days.

I never could figure out why a woman would want dead animals hanging around her neck, especially with those glassy eyes that seemed to stare right at me.

Finally, we all headed out the door carrying our Bibles and church offering envelopes.

When we arrived at church, we were supposed to head for our Sunday-school classes. Instead, my brother and I found one of our cousins and the three of us headed for a nearby cigar store to buy candy.

I bought myself one roll of Life Savers butter rum candy and one roll of Coffee Charms and managed to eat both before church was over. Sometimes we also visited a nearby pet store to study the fearsome creatures for sale there, like lizards and piranhas. All this made us late for Sunday school.

We often got into other mischief at church. Our new education building had a dumbwaiter, and once my brother decided to give me a ride in it. To my horror, the elevator got stuck between floors when a cable came off the track. One of the men in the church fixed it and got me out. I was grateful I wasn't hurt, and that he didn't tell my father about it!

Sometimes, we went into the second-floor bathroom and played a prank on the ladies walking outside. Many of them wore outlandish hats and we tried to land wet, wadded-up paper towels on those hats.

Now, in case you are thinking we were the church "brats," the minister's son was just as devilish. His behavior shocked even my brother and me!

A long church service followed Sunday school, and when we were older, my parents allowed us to sit in the balcony by ourselves. The church music often was too "long-hair" for us and we couldn't understand the sermons, so we were bored.

I ate my Coffee Charms and doodled on paper while my brother lay down in a pew and went to sleep.

One time after the service was over, I waited by our '54 Plymouth for my parents and began throwing snowballs at passing cars. I hit one quite hard and, to my surprise, the driver went around the block and came up behind me. He walked up to me and slapped me. It made quite an impression on me, but unlike kids today, I didn't even threaten to sue him.

Even though getting dressed up on Sundays was an ordeal and our behavior in church was sometimes awful, it was all worth it. Somehow, we learned many good things that remain with us today. And as for the pastor's son, he is an outstanding minister and president of a college! ❖

> *We were supposed to head for our Sunday-school classes. Instead, the three of us headed for a nearby cigar store to buy candy.*

Memories of a Country Church

By Pauline Corn

hen my thoughts drift back to people and places that were important to me during my formative years, I think of a little white church. In 1919, when I was child, we moved to a small community in the mountains of North Carolina. After having lived in town, it was a new and exciting experience to have woods and fields to explore, hills to climb and a creek to wade in, but what interested me most of all was the church that stood across the road from our house. It was a fairly large one-room frame structure with a belfry. The bell had such a loud, clear tone that it could travel the airwaves for many miles, reaching homes at the foot of the mountains and along the ridges. It rang out joyfully except when it tolled slowly and mournfully for a funeral.

There was no electricity in the church. It was lit by small kerosene lamps with shiny reflectors. They were held by brackets spaced at intervals along the walls. One time, during evening service, a lamp began to smoke and sputter. A man sitting near the end of the bench grabbed it and tossed it through an open window. Fortunately, it had been raining, so no harm was done when it exploded.

During the brief intermission between Sunday school and the preaching service, those wishing to quench their thirst went across the road to the pump in our backyard.

The small pedal organ and a few benches, for the choir singers, were grouped to the right of the pulpit. The organist was a young lady who lived on the side of one of the mountains we could see from our house. When weather permitted, she and her sisters made the long walk twice on Sundays and to midweek prayer meeting. I remember seeing them carry a lantern to light their way up the mountain. The singing leader was a tall, heavy-set man with a powerful voice. I can almost see him standing there by the organ, a shaped-note songbook in one hand and keeping time with the other. Sometimes he would suddenly switch from soprano to bass and his deep voice would drown out the other bass singers. He had studied music and sometimes went around holding singing schools at country churches. He conducted one at our church and that was my first instruction in music.

A large coal heater warmed the church. Sometimes it was necessary to replenish the fire during the sermon; then there would be the noisy distraction of coals being chunked up with the poker and the rattle of

coal as it was shoveled into the stove. One cold, windy morning before Sunday school, several of us were standing around the stove when Miss Sadie, one of the teachers, brushed against the stove and burned a hole in her new coat. She almost cried as she looked at the ugly charred spot. I felt like crying, too, for I knew she had saved butter and egg money for a long time so she could order that coat.

Sunday-school classes were conducted at certain benches assigned to them. It was rather noisy with so many talking at the same time. At the end of class, the superintendent tapped a bell, and the secretary stood and read the report of how many were present and the amount of collection for each class.

During the brief intermission between Sunday school and the preaching service, some went to the outside toilet behind the church. Since there was no water on the church grounds, those wishing to quench their thirst went across the road to the pump in our backyard.

During the years I attended church there, some of the pastors were educated men, but the first one I remember was an uneducated farmer who felt the Lord had called him to preach. But he was also of the opinion that a pastor should get out and earn his living. As an example, he cited the apostle Paul, who preached but earned his living by tent making. So he worked his farm during the week, and preached on Sundays. He and his wife, who always dressed in black from head to toe, were unfriendly, solemn-faced individuals. At first they drove a horse and buggy to church, but before his term as pastor was up, they bought a Model-T Ford. For some reason, he never learned to drive and his son had to do the chauffeuring.

I must admit that I was not very attentive during his long-winded sermons. Whenever possible, I liked to sit at the end of the bench by a certain window. There were more trees on that side of the church and I liked to watch the birds and squirrels.

Through a clearing in the woods, I could see a house way off in the distance. Threads of smoke from the chimneys and moving dots in the yard indicated that the house was occupied. I would sit and wonder about the people who lived there. Once, as I sat daydreaming, I was brought to swift and startled attention when the preacher suddenly gave the Bible a loud thump and thundered out, "This is God's Word. Are ye listenin'?" As his stern gaze swept over the congregation and seemingly came to rest on me, I shrank and felt guilty because I had not been paying attention.

When I first started attending church there, it was considered disrespectful to the Lord for anyone to pray while standing. Those called on to lead in prayer always knelt on the hard floor. There were loud "Amens" and "Hallelujahs" from some of the members. One dear old lady would sometimes get so happy she would clap her hands and shout. It scared me the first time I heard her for I thought she had taken sick and was crying out in pain.

I was deeply interested in music, so as we had no organ or piano then, at every opportunity I would slip over to the church and practice on the organ.

I have seen mothers breast-feed babies during service. Once, I sat by a mother who had tied a tiny bag of asafetida around her baby's neck, thinking it would ward off disease germs. It's a wonder the vile smell of the asafetida hadn't made the baby sick.

The church was not only a place to worship; it filled a social need as well. People seemed in no rush to get home after service, but stood around talking. There was no better place for young people to find sweethearts than at church, especially at the young people's meeting. Young men stood at the church door waiting to ask certain ladies if they might see them home. Often we children went home with friends, sometimes walking several miles; or else they would go home with us. The pastor always went home with someone for dinner. They liked to come to our house, for Mama was a good cook.

My favorite pastor was a man in his 30s who had attended Bible College. He and his plump wife were friendly and cheerful. They always shook hands and talked with us children. He knew how to make his sermons interesting and meaningful for us. For a while, his wife taught our Sunday-school class and we loved her. At Christmas she gave each girl in the class a small covered dish shaped like a hen sitting on a nest. I kept and treasured mine for years until it was broken.

A revival, or protracted meeting, was held in the fall, after crops were harvested. The visiting evangelist was expected to stay a night or two with different members of the church. Once he spent a night with us at the beginning of the revival, however, he liked his room and Mama's cooking so well, he decided to spend the rest of the time with us. It made more work for Mama, but she couldn't very well ask him to leave. It was at one of those meetings that I went to the "mourner's bench" and received Christ into my life.

At the close of the revival, a baptizing was held in the nearby creek. The pastor and evangelist believed in baptizing converts as soon as possible. We girls wore white middy suits and I remember how cold the water was. A family living near the creek let us use a bedroom heated by a fireplace for a dressing room. Later it was decided to hold baptizings in the summer when the water was not so cold.

At the close of the revival, a baptizing was held in the nearby creek. The pastor and evangelist believed in baptizing converts as soon as possible.

An event to look forward to was the annual Homecoming Day in August. As many of the former members as possible would come to the event. One year, a family drove all the way from western Nebraska in a Model-T and, in those days, that was quite a trip.

The day began with putting fresh flowers on all the graves. Then, after the 11 o'clock service at church, there was a dinner on the grounds. A long table had been made by placing planks over sawhorses. Ladies covered it with tablecloths and unloaded boxes and baskets of food. Then the pastor asked the blessing, and for the next hour or so, people ate, mixed and mingled and greeted friends from far and near.

Around 2 o'clock, the afternoon program got under way. It usually consisted of congregational singing, special music by visiting quartets and singing groups and a talk by a guest speaker. One year, the speaker was the church's first pastor. There was laughter in the congregation when he told about an amusing incident that had happened while he was pastor there.

One of the most affluent families in the church and community had invited him to spend the night at their home. When he arrived, the lady of the house greeted him at the front door and said, "I'm sorry, John isn't here just now; he had to go attend to a little business, but he said to tell you he'd be back directly. Now you sit out here on the porch where it's cool, while I finish churning."

But before he could sit down, there was the rattle of wheels on the road in front of the house. Thinking that it was John coming in, he stepped

down to the yard. Well, it was John all right, but he was in handcuffs, and the sheriff and a deputy were taking him to the county jail. They had caught him making moonshine somewhere up in the cove. No wonder the family was affluent.

When the program closed with the singing of *God Be With You Till We Meet Again,* and the last car had driven out of the churchyard, I always felt sad and lonely.

In those days there was little vandalism, and the church was often left unlocked. I was deeply interested in music, so as we had no organ or piano then, at every opportunity I would slip over to the church and practice on the organ. After much diligent practice, remembering what I had learned at singing school, I could finally play some of the easier songs. Later, when we had a

piano of our own, my dad, who had not known about my practicing at church, was amazed when I sat down and played a church song.

One day when I went to church to practice, out of curiosity, I looked in the closet where supplies were kept. To my surprise and delight, I found a "hidden treasure"—a shelf of books. I was an avid reader, so after that I divided my time between practice and delving into those musty volumes on many religious subjects. I remember reading the life story of Adoniram Judson, one of the early missionaries to India.

A few years ago a mysterious fire completely destroyed the old church. A long, low, modern-type structure was built near the old site. I seriously doubt that any little girl going there will look back, years from now, and find her church life as enjoyable as mine was. ❖

The Old Church-Bell Ringer

By the Rev. Ralph T. Schnarr

An old man with a boy one day
Went to see his place of love,
'Twas a church run down, neglected,
Before God summoned him above.
His heart was pierced with sorrow,
As he looked upon the place
Which was once his pride and glory,
But was now in sad disgrace.

"Come, my boy, set down a mite,
And I'll tell you a thing or two,
When I used to be the sexton,
Way back when hearts were true.
The graveyard's old and weedy
And the tombstone's toppled o'er;
Cattle are in it 'n' grazin';
It's makin' my heart sore.

"Mother and Dad are buried there,
And dear sweet Sally, too;
Fer 60 year, stayed by my side,
To struggle this life through;
We used to go to meetin',
Trudgin' 'long the dusty way,
But I never failed to ring the bell,
No matter how bad the day.

"After folk would cong'egate,
I'd see Sally in the choir;
A-singin' with the rest o' folk,
T'was always her heart's desire;
She seemed to sing above the rest,
Her voice was true and sweet,
Her shinin' face we loved to see,
'Cause she stayed at the Master's feet.

"Now my memory wanders back,
When we were young and gay,
When I was courtin' Sally,
We were happy every day.
We sat in church t'gether
And we sang the songs so free,
She would rest her hand in mine,
As we sang Abide With Me.

"Preachin' Bill, good man he was,
And though his pay was small,
Was doin' what he knew was right,
Answerin' the Master's call.
He did not tickle the people's ears
But preached the Gospel well,
And said if we we'n't livin' right,
We'd go right straight to hell.

"Son, those days are gone forever,
Now I am old an' gray,
I'm just a-stayin' out my time,
Then I will pass away;
If only I could ring the bell
To bring folk back to meetin'
And hear once more Ol' Preachin' Bill,
With his loud and noisy greetin'.

"Hear Sally and my mother sing,
Like angels sweet 'n true;
I'd gladly sacrifice a lot
To have them sing for you;
I was ne'er much a hand to sing,
No musician, folk'll tell.
I'm sure God'll be good to me,
'Cause I loved to ring the bell.

"Help me up them steps m' lad,
And lead me to the rope
Where I used to stand an' ring the bell,
I'll ring ag'in that sound of hope."
Clang! Clang! Clang! Clang!
"Sure is purty to my ears."
Clang! "Ain't that sweet, boy"
It fills my eyes with tears.

"Let's mosey down and rest a bit,
That ringin' has tired me so,
I'm mighty proud you brought me here,
But I allows we'd better go;

Years I've wished to see this place,
I knew I'd come somehow.
Thanks fer humorin' a po'er ol' man
To bring me here jus' now.

"LISTEN! Son, do you hear that voice,
That's a-singin' songs so sweet"
WHY! Why it's Sally, she sings fer me,
There on the golden street.
She's singin' a song I dearly love,
She's singin' Abide With Me,
The song that always fills my soul,
See, how good my Lord can be.

"WHY! Up there, too, are Mom and Dad,
Joinin' in the sweet refrain,
They're all singin' songs so blest,
I wish I too could sing;
There's jus' one thing that I can do,
The work I love so well,
To call folk to the meetin',
By the ringin' of the bell.

"Preachin' Bill and all the rest
Are busy on the other shore,
Singin' 'n' playin' lovely harps
Around the church-house door;
They don't seem quite so happy,
What it is I jus' can't tell;
They got a church and ever'thing,
And they even got a bell.

"LISTEN! The Lord is standin' up,
I'll tell what He has to say:
'We all are happy singin' songs,
Upon this our glorious day.
We can't go on just like this,
You have been busy I can tell,
You ALL play harps and sing the songs,
But no one to ring the bell.'

"'So John,' He tells me, 'Sonny,
We all do sing and play,
But there's no one to call the people
To church on service day;
And John, I know you're faithful.
On earth you served me well;
So come up here and help us,
Where you'll always ring the bell.'"

All Is Bright

By Esther L. Smith

In 1924, Christmas Eve was welcomed excitedly by the children of the Baptist Church of Suncook, N.H. Even the weather helped to make that Christmas memorable for a 7-year-old girl.

Pink afterglow colored the western sky as I set off down the street with my older sister. Our destination was the annual children's Christmas festivities at the church.

Mother had seen to it that I was well bundled. A heavy blue coat was slipped over my best wool dress; scarf and mittens were added, as well as the latest in winter fashion: a black beaver hat with wide ribbons hanging down back. Sturdy rubbers were drawn on over prized patent-leather slippers, taking care not to smudge my long, white, cotton stockings. Knowing I looked my best added to my rising anticipation.

The invigorating winter air was tinged with the fragrance of wood smoke as we hurried along. Streetlights were not yet on, but a glow had begun to appear in some windows. Snow crunched deliciously underfoot. Evergreen trees on the Colbys' lawn were frosted white and silhouetted against the sky, like teepees. Through the windows of a house near the street, a big tree loaded with gifts was visible. Then came the home of the grocer-baker; we youngsters liked him because he'd sell tiny 1-cent ice-cream cones to kids in strained circumstances.

The boys wore knickers and jackets, long dark stockings and high shoes. Some looked bandbox fresh, with slicked-down hair and shined shoes.

Twilight had deepened by the time we reached the church and the light was on over the door. Many young folks were trudging up the steps. (I was glad it was not a time when the big bell was rung, as it frightened me when it boomed as I came up the steps on Sunday morning.)

It was tradition in that church that Christmas Eve was for the young. A sweet-faced woman herded our group upstairs to the dining room. As we clumped up the worn treads, someone wailed, "Ouch! You stepped on my heel!"

The windows were steamed up and the room was filled with the buzz of shrill voices and the fragrance of cocoa. Someone called, "All ready, children!" There was a scramble for the long tables and the boys promptly forgot their manners, even though it was the last thing their mothers had instructed them about before they left home. Plates of sandwiches and mugs of the hot beverage caught their eyes, and the carefully arranged centerpieces were ignored.

I was too excited to eat much, and when gaily decorated cakes were brought out, there was an agonizing interval of indecision as I tried to choose. I had exercised great care not to spill cocoa on my dress.

While the others continued to eat, I got up and walked to the alcove that afforded a view of the sanctuary below. As I looked down on the deserted room, it seemed shadowy and unreal. The pews advanced stiffly up the aisle and the pipe organ gave off a dull glow in the shadows. I thought briefly of the pudgy boy who grudgingly hand-pumped the organ so his mother could play for services, and of the choir that sang each Sunday, standing in the loft to the right. We children watched, fascinated, sure that the lead soprano would choke sometime as she made up such faces on the high notes.

To the left of the pulpit, rising in grandiose splendor, was the tallest Christmas tree I had ever seen. It seemed to move slightly as tinsel and decorations gleamed and twinkled. It was capped with a stiff, regal star. I had been holding my breath, taking it all in. Then the janitor came in and started turning on lights, so I knew that the program would soon begin.

Turning from the alcove, I took in a mental picture of the group. The girls were really dolled up. Several had "crimped" their hair so that it stood out in unnatural kinks. Their dress ranged from average church garb to a satin party gown. The boys wore knickers and jackets, long dark stockings and high shoes.

Some looked bandbox fresh, with slicked-down hair and shined shoes. Others, equally well dressed, were already mussed up and their shoes were scuffed.

The sanctuary was filled with the pungent smell of the tree, warmed-over furnace air, and a trace of candy-bag goodies. I slipped into a seat with my friends. Adults were streaming in and sitting in the back.

Getting a closer look at the tree, my eyes went upward from cheesecloth bags filled with popcorn and candy to tissue-paper—covered packages of all shapes. A life-size candy cane, which looked like one I had seen at the Greek's candy kitchen, hung from a high branch.

My eyes stopped as I spied the doll. She was about 18 inches tall, arms outstretched, with real hair and lips parted in a faint smile, showing two pearly teeth. The movable eyes seemed to be looking right at me.

"Ooh, see the lovely doll!" I exclaimed to the girl next to me. My friend was busy talking and seemed not to notice. To this 7-year-old, the doll was the only thing on the tree. I got up from my seat and went back down the aisle to where Mother sat.

"Mama, do you see the doll with the blue dress?" I breathed.

"Yes, I guess I do. Now go back and sit down, dear," Mother answered matter-of-factly.

The concert began with singing, followed by

recitations. For the most part, they were well delivered, although there were the inevitable few who stood in painful forgetfulness. There were poems about Bethlehem, the Baby Jesus and a few about Santa Claus. I was thankful that I was in a dialogue with several girls and did not have to be on the platform alone.

After more singing, the Sunday-school superintendent called for quiet and said, "Boys and girls, I am sure that if you keep very still, you will hear Santa coming soon."

A breath-stopping silence fell, and sure enough, from way up in the belfry, there came a faint jingling of bells and the sound of hooves. A voice called, "Whoa, Dancer! Whoa, Prancer!"

The children were wiggling with excitement and faces of wonder turned toward the rear door as footsteps came down, nearer and nearer. Then the swinging doors opened with a swoop, and there stood Santa Claus, complete with pack.

"Hello, boys and girls!" he called in a strong voice.

"Hello, Santa!" was the deafening reply.

Santa progressed up the aisle, shaking hands with many adults and keeping up a steady chatter. He paused as he came to the children and put his hand on the head of a small boy. "Santa is so glad you are feeling better," he murmured to the boy, who had been dangerously ill. "My, how nice you all look."

A stepladder appeared out of nowhere to aid older boys in lifting down gifts. Santa called out names and had a message for each recipient. For a second, I thought about his voice; it sounded so much like Papa's.

Mr. Hedging (he looked like Andy Ump) was a favorite of the children and we all hooted and clapped when he pranced down the aisle with the large candy cane, the gift of an unknown admirer.

Suddenly I sat bolt upright. The doll was being handed to Santa. I could not help but envy the lucky girl who would get her. For some reason, Santa came down the aisle with the doll and stopped beside me.

"The card on this doll says, 'To Esther Smith.'" For just a second I could not breathe; then my arms were reaching. As the doll was passed, I noticed that Santa wore a ruby ring just like one my father wore. It had never occurred to me that the doll could be mine. The wonder of it was as great as the gift.

Soon the tree stood stripped of gifts and a welter of tissue paper covered the floor where the children sat. Santa said fond goodbyes and disappeared out the door. He could be heard climbing the stairs, still calling, "Merry Christmas!" Then he yelled, "On, Vixen, on, Blitzen!" and after a jingle of bells, all was silent.

A buzz of activity began as preparations were made to leave. A call for everyone to join in singing *Silent Night* calmed things down, and the strains of the beloved carol rose sweetly and thoughtfully through the group. Clasping my doll, I sang with a love I had never felt before for the wee Christ Child.

Turning to leave, I saw my father enter the back of the room and wondered where he had been. One of the big boys said smartly, "Hello, Santa," but Father paid no attention to him. Santa? Santa!

A tide of circumstances added up for me. Santa's voice was strong, like Papa's; his ruby ring was just like Papa's; and his attention to each child, his kindness—so like Papa! My knees felt weak, but not from disappointment. I had known for some time that Christmas meant more than a brightly garbed man bringing gifts. Who better to be Santa than my dear Papa?

Going home under the luminous sky, one star seemed to glow more brightly than the others, sending long rays on all sides, and it added to the hushed walk in the snapping cold. I cradled the doll in one arm and held tightly to Mama's hand. An important step had been taken and I sensed the change. Feeling warm and secure and wishing all children might find their Papa was Santa, I thought of the birthday to be celebrated on the morrow and softly hummed: "All is calm, all is bright." ❖

My Most Memorable Christmas

By Irene A. Bradshaw

All Christmases are special. Selecting one, which is most memorable, is difficult. Looking down yesterday's road through a rear-view mirror, I must stop in the 1920s. I was 9 years old, the fifth in a family of seven children. Mother had chosen me to accompany her to midnight Mass, an honor bestowed on only one of us each Christmas Eve. Just being alone with her, not having to share her company with my brothers and sisters, was exciting in itself.

It was a clear, crisp night in below-zero weather. Drifts were piled high; the air was still. A black velvet sky held a million stars. The only sound was the squeaking crunch of our footsteps on the packed snow as we walked, arm in arm, the six blocks to St. Patrick's church in Eau Claire, Wis. Our breath formed white frost on the woolen scarves wrapped around our coat collars.

Upon arrival, we went first to the side altar. The nuns had fashioned the manger scene using life-size figures, banked by fresh evergreen boughs. The piney scent filled the church. As I knelt beside the crib, I was one with the Wise Men and the shepherds. To me, this was the night the Infant was born, and I was there.

The Mass was special, with the choir singing Christmas hymns and the sermon brief and inspiring. Outside on the church steps, smiles and handclasps and "Merry Christmas!" greetings were exchanged, and then a fast walk home in even colder air.

It was a good feeling to crawl into the warm bed I shared with my younger sister. I still marvel that she didn't even murmur when my cold feet touched against her. Not even the anticipation of an exciting Christmas Day could keep me awake for long.

Ah, yes, it was a memorable Christmas indeed! ❖

Hark! The Herald Angels Sang

By Evelyn Miller

Christmas was upon me again. In the living room, standing proudly, was a small tree, magnificent with several vintage ornaments (a few last remnants of childhood Christmases), colored lights and, on the top, a rather bedraggled angel.

Modern electric lights in colors sprayed radiance among the furry branches of the small, long-needled tree—my tree of choice, now that I am widowed, with children grown and gone. And suddenly, I didn't see my modern tree at all—but another, earlier version.

I see the tree of my childhood. I am 10 years old and the year is 1924. I am very excited, for it is Christmas Eve. I am walking through deep snow, and the swirling, soft flakes touch my hot cheeks. I toss back my stylish, carefully rolled finger curls and brush the snowflakes from my eyelashes as I continue to wend my way from the very end of Fifth Street, where I live, on the south side of our small city of Grand Haven, Mich.

Upon reaching the corner of Franklin Street and Fifth, I abruptly turn left. One more block to go.

Ah, there it is, barely visible now in the thickening flurry of the soft snowflakes—the church of my childhood, the St. John's Evangelical Lutheran Church of my German ancestors. I am the youngest member of the family in the church of my elders.

My fingers tingle, my cheeks grow more rosy and my heart pounds. It is Christmas Eve.

My fingers tingle, my cheeks grow more rosy and my heart pounds. It is Christmas Eve, and Christmas Eve is not only the night to usher in the birth of

Jesus in our small parish, but an evening of unforgettable treats.

As I shyly enter the church, I wistfully look for a place that will give me a complete view of the glorious, towering Christmas tree. My heart almost stops. There it is, in the corner, directly to the right of the tall pulpit at which I hardly dare glance; from it come sermons of such intensity that I cringe inwardly and the gold tassels on the blue velvet paraments seem to shake. But tonight should bring a gentler message—the birth of Christ.

I cannot swallow as I gaze with wonder upon the giant tree. It spans the beams above. Glistening garlands circle it in dignity. And ah, the candles—beautiful, real candles held in metal cups, standing proudly lighted, interspersed among the prickly branches.

I take my seat and humbly bow my head in prayer. The service begins with the songs I've grown to love, aided by the small choir—*Silent Night; Hark, the Herald Angels Sing, Oh, Little Town of Bethlehem.* As my voice peals out in childish notes, I am filled with glory, and still the best is yet to come.

The minister takes his rightful place in the tall pulpit and once more we bow in prayer. Although his message is vibrating, inspired and dedicated, and the old story, new once more, is thrilling, an anticipatory chill runs through me.

Christmas treat time is next! As each child's name is called, that child solemnly takes his place at the front of the church, directly to the left of the tree. One of the elders brings forth a large pack, and one by one, the children file by as their names are called out.

I almost faint as I realize that I am next. Timidly reaching forth, I am given a small cardboard box filled with hard candies. Lovely Christmas designs are emblazoned on the small box and a tiny red cord string is attached to the top … but there is more!

A mammoth, spicy, dark orange is put into my eager hands. Ah, how the smell permeates the air! My mouth waters.

It's more than "Merry Christmas" that I am wishing you. It's "Bright and Happy Every Day" the coming twelve months through.

I go back to my seat and place the candy and orange next to me, for the festivities are not yet over. The more theatrical children who know no shyness now step forward, one by one, and speak Christmas verses. I am next to the last and I can hardly wait, for I love any type of theatrics.

I am the only one given a Christmas verse with gestures, and joyously I raise my hand, pointing while declaring, "Yonder lies, under the Star of Bethlehem, the crib containing the Baby Jesus." When I speak the name "Baby Jesus," my arms softly form a circle and I mentally hold the tiny Baby in my eager arms.

There is applause and it delights me, for then I know I have put my verse over, and it is appreciated and felt. I have made my small contribution to wonderful Baby Jesus and His miraculous birth. I go back and sit down.

Another prayer is offered up after the Christmas collection plate has been passed, and then the final hymns roll forth in beautiful, rich, vibrant tones as the rolling sounds of the church organ accompany the singers … Triumphant! Triumphant!

Putting my coat on and my woolen cap and gloves and scarf, I anxiously feel for my "treasures" and, grasping them, I leave. When I go out the front door, I once more turn and lovingly survey the triumphant, giant Christmas tree with its flickering candles casting shadows upon the darkened interior.

The snow is now coming down in heavy swirls. Pushing ahead eagerly, I make my way faster and faster back through the footsteps made by others ahead of me.

Turning the corner to the right on Franklin Street, I remake my former steps, in reverse this time. As I approach Washington Street, I glance up at the town clock, which is softly striking the hour of 10 p.m.

Bells are ringing … the snow is drifting and a feeling of supreme ecstasy comes over me … it is heavenly.

And, thus it was—Christmas Eve, 1924. ❖

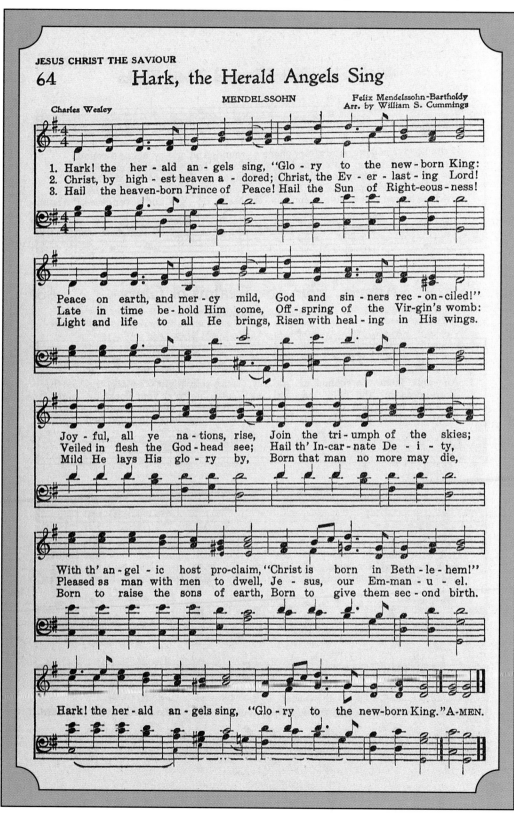

The Tribute

By Richard C. Morgan

Beneath the puffy, wispy clouds
(Those spangles of the sky),
Stands a little wooden church,
Which lived in days gone by.

Once it had a preacher,
Who taught the Word of God,
To members—who said, "AMEN!"
And to sleepers who would nod.

Women brought their dinners,
Food you'd not surpass,
And singing was contagious,
Like the chiggers in the grass.

Always, there was fellowship,
Among "the faithful few,"
Standing in the churchyard,
In a Sunday-morning dew.

Let those who pass this church house
Please remember when
It was always just and proper
To go to church back then.

A tribute to our Maker,
On whom its saints would call,
May it stand forever,
And never, ever fall.

PERSIS CLAYTON WEIRS
1998

Preachers We Knew

An old anecdote from the annals of country churches goes something like this: John, a wizened farmer and notoriously known as a man of few words, pulled up to the small stone church. He unloaded his children—his wife was ill—and went inside to hear the Word of the Lord. After the obligatory hymns and other accoutrements of the service, the farmer pulled up a pew as the country preacher began the sermon.

The preacher started slowly, but before the hour was up he had doffed jacket and tie, rolled up sleeves and worked into a frenzied sweat. He preached long, loud and eloquently from the Good Book, attacking the works of the devil and exhorting his flock by many words to eschew evil.

Farmer John shook the pastor's hand and nodded quietly, barely uttering a word as he left the country church with his brood. Back at the farm John's wife wanted to know how the service had gone.

"Was there a big crowd?" she asked.

"Yup."

"Did Brother Dave preach the message?"

"Yup."

"What did he preach on?"

"Sin."

"Well," she asked, exasperated, "what did he say?"

"He's agin it."

Brother Dave and all the preachers I knew in the Good Old Days were "agin" sin in all its forms. They preached robustly on the evils of liquor, gambling, dancing and carousing. But in those days preachers were more than just a Sunday morning diversion. They were our neighbors and friends. They shared Sunday dinner with us and many times worked shoulder to shoulder in our fields during harvest season.

No one man ever had more influence on my life, spiritually speaking, than Brother Tom. He and his wife, Pat, took over the pastorate at our small church when Janice and I were newlyweds. A young lay minister myself, I learned the fine art of preaching at Brother Tom's feet, not in some seminary. I led the congregational hymns, preached occasionally and assisted in baptisms—all under Tom's ever watchful and sage eye.

I'll never forget the time a drought-driven forest fire threatened Brother Tom's home as the weekend approached. Several of us from the congregation had tried to clear a firebreak far enough from the house to protect it, but the heat-driven winds kept blowing firebrands closer and closer as the flames worked their way around the mountainside.

Tom, a devout man and believer in miracles, came to me and said he didn't want his congregation working to save the house on the Lord's Day. "The scriptures say, 'Remember the sabbath day, to keep it holy,'" he said. "If the only way we'll save the house is to work on the Sabbath, I'll let the flames have it. I'm going to pray for rain."

Pray he did, and rain it did. A small cloud on the horizon soon boiled into a thunderhead. A hard deluge knocked the fire to its knees. A gentle rain through the night cooled the last embers. And, as a side benefit, the drought cycle had ended. All due to the faith of one country preacher.

I know you'll enjoy these stories of preachers we have known. They remember the best of men like Brother Tom who were our friends, our neighbors, our teachers and spiritual mentors back in the Good Old Days.

—Ken Tate

The Preacher & the Penny Candy

By Beulah M. Morain

When the new storekeeper insisted on keeping his store open on the Lord's day, he found folks were willing to put wheels on their convictions.

"Yes sir! You heard right; we've bought ourselves a hardware business." Mr. Lawson wiped his hands on his white cotton butcher's apron as he walked around the meat counter. He handed Papa the package wrapped in white butcher paper.

"The new owners will move into our old house. They've bought our home and store, stock, fixtures and accounts. They will be doing a little painting and repairs. They plan on adding some things we haven't carried before, but there won't be any shutdown time.

"We're moving a couple miles down the highway. Our hardware business is right on the highway and our home is just around the corner from it. We'll be looking for you to come by and visit us."

The announcement came as a total surprise to me. Lawson's Grocery was a neighborhood landmark. It had always been across the road from our little community church.

Mrs. Lawson must have read the hurt and surprise from the look on my face. She slipped her arm around my waist from where she sat in her high-backed wooden rocking chair.

All our eyes were on the windows of the house across the street. All the people were hoping to get another look at our newest neighbors.

"It's okay, Honey. We're not moving far. You can walk over and visit with me anytime. I'll be home, or you can come see me at the store, same as here."

Mrs. Lawson was a plump, gray-haired, grandmotherly lady. She had the confidence of all the neighborhood girls. On hot summer afternoons, she would listen to all our pains and problems. She would help us with our hair ribbons and plait our hair in braids for us. She would advise us if we asked, but never condemned us. We looked on her as our friend.

About two weeks later, I watched the Lawsons pack their furniture into a truck to move to their new home. Mr. Lawson continued to bring Mrs.

Lawson to the store. He would stay just long enough to arrange the fresh meat in the counter before heading for his new business.

Mrs. Lawson continued to keep the neighborhood grocery open six days a week. The vacant house next-door was a constant reminder that our friend had moved away, leaving us to strangers.

There was a high degree of excitement a few days later when a large moving van appeared at the vacant house. The neighbor ladies peeked from behind lace curtains. They talked at length across backyard fences. Boys in patched overalls climbed high in nearby trees to get a better look.

We crept inside in disbelief. The pennies burned hot in my pocket. I eyed the candy case. Pennies were for the Sunday-school offering, not candy every week.

We girls gathered early for our midweek junior mission circle. We sat on the church steps to watch as the movers brought in some of the most beautiful furniture we had ever seen. During the Depression of the '30s, we had become accustomed to threadbare sofas with sagging springs, apple-box shelves and mattresses stuffed with corn shucks or straw.

We discussed how "they" must be very rich. "They" were coming to us from some big city "back East."

The following Sunday, Sunday school was just over and children who were going home still chatted in the churchyard. The families who were staying for church had just found their pews. The pianist played Onward Christian Soldiers as the choir filled the choir loft. Across the street, a large black car stopped in front of the store. A short, spectacled man, a dour-faced woman and a young girl with curly brown hair got out. They looked around for a minute before disappearing into the vacant house.

Brother Ferguson had a difficult time holding our attention that Sunday morning. All our eyes were on the windows of the house across the street. All the people were hoping to get another look at our newest neighbors.

I could hardly wait for Monday morning to come. It would be my turn to go to the grocery store for my mother. As I rounded the corner by the store, Mr. Lawson was unloading paint from his hardware truck. Men on ladders were scraping the outside of the weather-beaten store building.

Mr. Seamier, the new owner, was overseeing the men assembling long glass cases. His wife carried buckets of soapsuds to clean and scrub the wooden shelves. On the window seat, near the large front window, sat the girl with the brown curly hair. She was playing with her Shirley Temple doll. Her neatly combed hair, immaculate dress, polished black shoes and white ankle socks made me feel shabby.

I stood facing her for several minutes. She ignored me as she continued to brush her doll's hair. I waited, shifted my feet, coughed and drew a line in the dust on the floor with my big toe.

"I'd like to be your friend," I finally said, abruptly.

"What do you want, young lady?" her mother questioned. She looked hard at my faded, tattered dress as she took the grocery list from my dusty hand.

"We've always taught our little girl that cleanliness is next to godliness," her mother quoted. She handed me the paper bag and escorted me to the front door.

Tears stung my eyes as I walked several blocks home. I set the grocery bag on the kitchen table before I ran upstairs. I flung myself across the bed and cried into my pillow. The rest of that week, I would walk by the store, but wouldn't go inside.

The next Sunday morning, my sisters and I left early for Sunday school. I was dressed in my best dress with a few pennies tied in the corner of my handkerchief. These were tucked away, out of sight, in my pocket. We stood outside and pressed our faces against the cool glass of the store window to look inside.

The appearance of the store had changed during that week. There were still products for the table: flour, salt, cornmeal, oatmeal, potatoes, dried apples, raisins, dried peas and, of course, dried beans. There was a new cracker barrel and a great round cheese. Where Mrs. Lawson's rocker had been, the new owner had put in three long glass cases to form a U-shaped counter. A short wooden door closed the back against intruders. A shiny new cash register sat on the top of the front case.

The shelves on one side of this counter contained an offering to feminine vanity: silk ribbons, lace, buttons, pins, needles, thread and hand mirrors. The other side held the gentlemen's choices: pipes, tobacco, cigars, shaving mugs with brushes, pocket combs and tie clips.

Facing the front window, the case was filled with candy in large glass jars. Different colors of lollipops, black licorice twists, red-and-white peppermint sticks, brown horehound drops, pale yellow lemon drops and Gibraltars—white candies about 3 inches long and as hard as the rock for which they were named—were all displayed in full view.

As we leaned our foreheads against the glass, several other children joined us. We pressed our noses against the glass and feasted our eyes on the array of candy.

Mr. Seamier walked from his house, crossed the lawn, put his key in the lock and opened the door of the store. He switched on the light in the

John Slobodnik

candy case, then walked to the back of the store. Soon the meat counter light came on and the new ceiling fan started to hum.

"Come right in." Mr. Seamier smiled as he spoke to us.

"On Sunday?" we all chorused.

"Of course; there is nothing special about Sunday. It just depends on the day of the week that you choose to worship," he observed.

We crept inside in disbelief. The pennies burned hot in my pocket. I eyed the candy case. Candy! Papa sometimes brought us a little candy home at the first of the month, but Papa's meager wages didn't allow for much luxury. Pennies were for the Sunday-school offering, not candy every week.

Nervous fingers untied the white handkerchief. Other dusty fingers dug deep into overall pockets. Copper pennies began to appear on the glass countertop. They disappeared into the big cash register as, one after another, we made our choices.

As Roy Brown, the Sunday-school superintendent, rang the final bell, a dozen children trooped into the church with full mouths but empty pockets. Not a word was said, but all eyes were downcast during the offering. All the children's classes were very quiet that morning.

At the close of the morning service, the preacher stood at the church door. He shook hands with all the members. "Thank you for coming," he said. "See you next Lord's day.

"Now, Brother Brown, you and I need to pay a visit to our newest neighbor," he concluded.

Mr. Seamier was sitting on the cracker barrel and reading the morning newspaper when the two men entered the store. "I'm Roscoe Ferguson," the preacher said as he extended his hand. "This is our Sunday-school superintendent, Roy Brown."

Mr. Seamier rose, folded his paper, and peered over his glasses at the two men who had just entered. "What can I do for you gentlemen?" he asked.

"It seems, my good man, that certain of our children were entrusted with offerings by their parents which failed to appear in the offering plate. It was robbing God when you took that money from those innocent children."

"I fail to agree with you gentlemen," Mr. Seamier said. "I didn't force any child to make a purchase. They were waiting outside for me to open the store. Many of my former customers, in a more progressive city, found it a convenience to be able to shop on Sunday. I had no qualms about selling to the children today. I plan to continue to keep my store open seven days a week. People will soon come to expect it."

"As you see fit, sir. Let me remind you that one of our members, Mr. Chapman, owns a grocery store about a mile down the highway. I'll gladly take my neighbors there to shop if you insist on this," Mr. Brown declared with conviction. "I'm confident that a tithe of that money will be returned to God in our house of worship."

"Think it over, Brother, you'll be trading dimes for dollars," the preacher echoed.

As children, we were disappointed to see no lights on in the candy store the next Sunday morning. No keys turned in the lock on the door at the store. No spectacled man sat on the cracker barrel to read the morning paper.

When the subject of tithing is discussed, or the preacher uses the text from Malachi 3:8–10, I'm still reminded of the preacher, the children and the penny candy in that little country store during the Depression. ❖

THE CHURCH
142   Onward, Christian Soldiers
ST. GERTRUDE

Sabine Baring-Gould   Arthur S. Sullivan

1. On-ward, Christian sol-diers, March-ing as to war, With the cross of Je - sus
2. Like a might-y ar - my Moves the Church of God; Brothers, we are tread-ing
3. Crowns and thrones may perish, Kingdoms rise and wane, But the Church of Je - sus
4. On-ward, then, ye peo - ple, Join our hap-py throng, Blend with ours your voic-es

Go - ing on be-fore: Christ the roy-al Mas-ter Leads a-gainst the foe;
Where the saints have trod; We are not di - vid - ed, All one bod-y we,
Con-stant will re-main; Gates of hell can nev - er 'Gainst that Church prevail;
In the tri-umph song; Glo - ry, laud, and hon - or Un - to Christ the King;

For-ward in-to bat - tle, See, His banners go.
One in hope and doc - trine, One in char-i - ty.   Onward, Christian sol - diers,
We have Christ's own promise, And that cannot fail.
This through countless a - ges Men and an-gels sing.

REFRAIN

March-ing as to war, With the cross of Je-sus Go-ing on be-fore. A-MEN.

Our Beloved Pied Piper

By Elizabeth Francois

*L*ooking back to the beginning of the century in my old home town, I can see myself again as a little girl, together with my small playmates, trailing happily after our visiting priest, Father Cleary, our "Pied Piper."

Tall pines guarded our small sawmill town in northern Wisconsin. Rows of identical barn-red houses climbed the hill like cheap red stones in the platinum setting of the beautiful woods and lakes.

There were only three pure-white houses in town—one for the company doctor, one for the town superintendent and the largest for the owner of the town who came only occasionally to check his holdings. He was a rather corpulent lumber tycoon who also owned a large furniture factory in another large city. A wooden fence in front of each house gave the occupants a sense of privacy and wooden sidewalks with their wide cracks provided a never-ending treasure hunt for the children.

Before putting the children to bed early, the little girls' hair was put up in rags, hopefully for long curls.

The townspeople, except for a very few French and Irish Catholics, were mostly of Norwegian and Swedish extraction. Men worked long hours for meager pay and a Catholic church and regular pastor were not to be dreamed of.

The McGees, with their eight children, were considered the backbone of the Catholic congregation. It was plump little Mrs. McGee who notified the bishop of our plight and offered her home as a place to hold Mass and confessions and to house the priest for his short stay.

So it was that Father Cleary was assigned as our mission priest. He came once a month to perform his duties.

When word was received that he was coming, the McGees tacked a sign up in the company store, stating the time and place of services. This was the highlight of the month in the uneventful lives of the Catholic people of our town.

Children would empty their piggy banks to help with the collection. A week in advance, Mama McGee would start to clean her house. Everything must be spotless for Father's visit. Curtains would be washed and stretched, blankets and sheets laundered, and the sitting room rug would be scrubbed. Other Catholic women would donate home-baked goods and hot dishes to make Father's table deserving of his visit. The one linen tablecloth, a wedding present, was brought out from mothballs and washed and ironed until it shone like satin.

The night before Father's arrival, the galvanized washtub was brought in from the shed, and after heating water from the big rain barrel, Mama McGee scrubbed the smallest ones until they were red. Papa McGee cut the boys' hair, soup-bowl style, the only way he knew how. Before putting the children to bed early, the little girls' hair was put up in rags, hopefully for long curls.

Father Cleary arrived at noon on Saturday on the one train of the day, dubbed "the Toonerville Trolley." It was probably the slowest train he ever rode. He was met by all but the band, and treated with the reverence of a pope.

Confessions were heard Saturday night in the darkened bedroom off the sitting room, behind the heavy, dark green drapes with the large ball fringe. Children came with their simple sins, probably nothing more serious than disobedience—maybe lingering too long on a summer's night, playing pompom-pull-away under the big arc light in front of the old red boardinghouse.

The small congregation filed in on Sunday morning, each in his Sunday best, and took seats on the straight wooden chairs in the sitting room. The long library table in the center of the room served as an altar. The starched white scarf with the wide crocheted edge looked strangely chaste on this day. Holy candles that Mama McGee always had on hand in case of sickness were placed in glass candleholders and lit for the service. Vases of wildflowers graced the setting.

Timmy and Tommy, the 9-year-old McGee twins, were chosen to serve as altar boys. The night before Mass, Father Cleary instructed the boys briefly in the duties of serving Mass. With a few meaningful nods and gestures, the boys did all right. They looked deceptively angelic in their white shirts and black bow ties, even if they didn't have the accustomed surplices and cassocks.

The 3- and 4-year-olds, so innocent of what was really taking place, thought it was all such fun. They stole impish glances at one another, then hid their faces behind chubby hands to smother a forbidden giggle. Nothing escaped the eyes of the parents and the frowns on their faces and their tightly pursed lips gave the children fair warning of what to expect when they got home.

Papa McGee lead the congregation in singing familiar and much-loved hymns a cappella. His strong tenor voice, so full of feeling, moved the parishioners.

People sat in rapt attention as Father gave his sermon, so hungry were they to hear the Word of God. There were no stained-glass windows, no padded kneeling benches, no pipe organ or trained choir, but God was there, and as the sun streamed in through the lace curtains, it was as if God was smiling on us all.

Everyone except the smallest children received communion, returning to their seats to kneel awhile in thanksgiving for all the blessings and grace received.

With the final blessing of the priest, Mass was over for the month. Father shook the hand of every adult present and patted the heads of the children, giving each a holy card in remembrance of him.

When Father Cleary departed for his return trip, he looked like the Pied Piper with all of the children trailing after him to the station. As he boarded the train, he turned to bless the little ones. He would come again to brighten the lives of his people. For the time being, the song was ended, but the melody lingered on. ❖

The Congregation Was Tipsy

By Joseph S. Hufham

It happened in September 1910. For days, newspapers had been reporting that Haley's Comet was on its way. The Hugh MacRae Company of Wilmington had bought a lot of land in Columbus County and was making an attempt to colonize it with Germans.

At the same time, Shed Mitchell was having a large sawmill built at the western edge of the village. The MacRae Company had the village name changed from Roberson, N.C., to New Berlin, in remembrance of Berlin, Germany, and Mitchell named his organization The New Berlin Lumber Company.

Among others moving into the community was my father, the Rev. N.D. Hufham, who had been ordained to preach by the Cheerful Hope Baptist Church pastor and deacons, 7 miles southwest of New Berlin. He came to the sawmill village to put up a market, and he found no church in the village. However, eight members of the Cheerful Hope and the Living Chapel section had moved to New Berlin.

With their help, Papa got busy. They rented a shell of a house that had been built by a German named Clinger who had quit farming and gone back north. Papa had the partitions torn out of the Clinger house; they had been made of wide, rough boards, and he made benches of them.

Then he got the Rev. I.A. Cains, from Chadbourn, N.C., (once the strawberry capitol of the world), to help him conduct a revival. They alternated—one preaching one night, and one the next. There were no radios, no televisions, no theater—no places of amusement at all—and so the improvised house of worship was filled every night.

Meanwhile, Carroll had made so much cider that it was getting hard, and developed the kick of a wild mule.

Papa took advantage of the occasion and organized a Sunday school. For a while, M.A. Brodeaux, a charter member of the church to be organized, was superintendent. There was a good man of the community by the name of Wright Carroll, and the second year he was made superintendent.

By now, the faithful wanted a church building. Shed Mitchell let them have lumber. Arthur Herring and Jack Hufham contracted the building. Up went the church. At the same time, Wright Carroll decided to build a rough-board store where he'd sell furniture, and he had a corner cut off to sell cider. He sold it from kegs set upon the counter for 5 cents a glass.

At first, his cider was sweet, though it acted on some as a purgative. A fellow just couldn't drink enough to get tipsy, but it was a great place to practice fellowshipping, and brethren coming in from work evenings would drop over, have a cider, and stand around and talk.

Carroll did not tolerate boisterous or profane language and the men respected him for it. B.F. Applewhite had gotten the town incorporated that year and they'd made Carroll policeman on standby. Meanwhile, Carroll had made so much cider that it was getting hard, and developed the kick of a wild mule.

It was about this time that news circulated that Haley's Comet was coming and the tail would sweep the earth. T.W. Pridgeon was the A.C.L. railroad operator at New Berlin and folks took to gathering at the depot to learn if he'd picked up any news about the comet.

Finally, the date was determined when the comet could be seen with the naked eye. Patrons of the grog shop went there immediately after supper for a cider and neighborly conversation. Carroll had just tapped a keg of hard cider, and by the time a man finished his first glass, he began feeling good. The second made him tipsy.

All hands had just had the second round, waiting to see the comet, when a young man ran in calling, "The comet is coming! It is visible in the sky. Pridgeon (the operator) says that he had picked up news that the tail might sweep the earth." All hands piled out to see the comet.

The steps up to Papa's shop were made of heavy planks, 16 feet long. He closed his market, walked out, and sat down on the steps. I was 8 years old. I stood in the yard watching the comet; it looked round and yellow, with a tail like a well-worn house broom.

Back at the grog shop, some of the men wondered aloud if they were doing the right thing, drinking while on the verge of being swept into eternity. It wasn't long before two walked the three blocks to sit on the steps close to Papa, expressing their hope that they wouldn't get swept away if they were with a preacher.

Papa spoke to them at once about being ready, "for ye know not the day nor the hour that the Son of Man cometh."

Others at the grog shop got the same idea as the first two. It wasn't long before all of Carroll's patrons were on the steps at Papa's shop, listening to him talk. Finally Carroll himself showed up and sat quietly to listen to the Gospel.

I kept looking at the comet, then listening to Papa preach about how the world would be eventually purged by fire.

Some of the men were so tipsy they could hardly sit up, but all kept quiet to listen to the Word. There must have been 20 in Papa's "congregation" that night, and they stayed until past midnight. By then all had decided the comet wasn't going to sweep everyone away after all, so all hands went back to Carroll's shop for a bracer before going to their respective homes and to beds.

If I recall right, Papa's next sermon was about how getting scared into religion at a moment of crisis just doesn't work. It didn't appear to work on that occasion, but it must have been comforting to tipsy congregation at the time. ❖

Two Sides to Pounding the Preacher

By Lydia Singleton Miller

When I was a child, our church was the center of social life in the rural South. Pounding the preacher was one of our most enjoyable affairs, filled as it was with suspense, surprise and bountiful servings of refreshments.

One night soon after a new minister had moved into our midst, guests would just happen to drop by, each pretending surprise at seeing all the others as they added their pound of gifts to the pile on the kitchen table. Guests brought refreshments, too, and the minister's wife, completely taken by surprise, bustled about excitedly, helping with the serving.

Both gifts and refreshments were geared to the season. I remember one autumn especially, when the pungent odor of gift apples mingled with the aroma of the hot chocolate and coffee we were served with coconut and chocolate cakes.

In addition to pounds of apples, there were tomatoes, cabbage, turnips, onions, home-canned vegetables and jellies. There were eggs, chickens, home-cured hams and shoulders, and a couple of flitches of bacon. Obviously these weighed much more than a pound, but plenty of pounds of butter showed up.

After the pounding, according to the PK, there were apples to can, sauerkraut to be made, and a week's diet of turnips rather than let anything spoil.

There was the usual debate about which was heavier, a pound of feathers or a pound of gold, but with the scarcity of gold, the subject usually veered off to iron or lead. When one guest brought a feather pillow, another, our blacksmith, produced his gift, a hitching weight that he had poured. (A hitching weight was an iron, usually flat on one side and rounded over the top, with an embedded ring. It was used in lieu of a hitching rack or pole. Anyplace a driver wanted to stop, he could hitch his horse or team by dropping the weight to the ground after he had looped the reins through the ring.)

The gifts demonstrated much ingenuity. One merchant's pound was of buttons, with a generous sprinkling of shoe buttons, both white and black, complete with a couple of shoe buttonhooks. Those buttons and hooks were much appreciated, as the minister had seven children, and the loss of a shoe button posed a problem. Buttoning high-button shoes without a shoe hook was well near impossible.

As I grew older, preacher pounding gradually gave way to the more sedate, and perhaps more suitable reception for the new minister and his family in the church dining room. It was rare to hear of a pounding after the late 1920s.

At a recent reception, I was bemoaning the passing of the colorful Preacher Pounding in the Good Old Days when a little senior citizen said, "Well do I remember them, I'm a minister's daughter, a PK, as preacher's kids call themselves today. And how we used to dread those poundings!"

She told how every evening the children had to get into company clothes and their shoes, when they had much rather have gone barefoot, or better still, gone to bed, but they never knew what evening company would just drop by.

Sometimes a goodly soul would tip the family off as to when to expect the pounding, and that was truly a godsend, but, expected or not, it was proper to be surprised.

After the pounding, according to the PK, there were apples to can, sauerkraut to be made, and a week's diet of turnips rather than let anything spoil. The gifts were most welcome, however, as minister's salaries were meager, at best, but some posed problems.

One little girl brought a motto, "The Lord loveth a cheerful giver," painstaking cross-stitched in white on bright red. Should the minister put the motto up on the wall? Would members take it as a hint? But if it was not displayed, the little girl would be disappointed.

Nothing was ever wasted. If gifts couldn't

be used, they were stored, and at the next parish, donated to the church bazaar, and the size of the pounding was a gauge of the new congregation's generosity.

Many gifts were treasured, as were friendships formed at the pounding and that lasted a lifetime. "One gift," the little senior citizen PK said, "was a little portable organ. It was an answer to prayer. I'd always wanted one. Lo, I received it at our last preacher pounding. It is one of my treasured possessions from the Good Old Days." And so are my memories. ❖

Mama Fed the Preacher

By Elzena A. Scott

I wonder now how the minister ever managed to preach his evening sermon after one of my mother's company dinners!

I grew up on a farm in eastern Washington state during the 1920s, and although we had no money, we ate well. About all my mother ever bought was baking powder and vanilla from the Watkins man or the Raleigh man who made monthly visits in the truck. Everything else was homegrown.

We lived 6 miles from the nearest town, but my parents rarely missed a Sunday morning church service. During the summer, we went in the Model-T Ford; in the fall, when the roads turned to mud, we went by horse and buggy. After the first snowfall, we traveled by sleigh.

Our congregation did not vote on our ministers; they were appointed. Evidently their terms of service were short, because I can recall a succession of pastors, and as soon as each pastor and his family arrived, my mother religiously invited them to a Sunday dinner.

Entertaining the preacher and his family was a special occasion and my mother always outdid herself. There was fried chicken, of course, and rich gravy, mashed potatoes, homemade noodles, and corn (either canned or fresh on the cob), fruit salad mixed with heavy whipped cream and an assortment of pickles.

Then, when we thought we couldn't swallow another bite, Mother would bring out the pies. I wonder now how the minister ever managed to preach his evening sermon after one of my mother's company dinners!

After that, Mother's duty was done, but the minister's duties were just beginning. One of them was to make periodic visits to encourage the members of his congregation.

I don't recall that we were ever forewarned, and he always arrived close to the noon hour. His purpose was twofold: He was guaranteed a good meal, and it was the only time when he could visit with my father, a busy farmer who came home for dinner promptly at noon.

I still recall my mother's reaction when the minister drove into our yard, his Model-T loudly announcing his arrival. Mother would exclaim, "Mercy! Here comes the preacher!"

Then she would rush into her bedroom, snatch off her soiled apron and quickly replace it with a clean one.

Next, she would remove a hairpin or two and try to catch up the wisps of hair that had escaped the bun on the top of her head. Then, flustered but smiling, she would go to the door to welcome her pastor.

The visitor was invited into the seldom-used parlor and Mother would attempt to entertain him, at the same time wondering nervously how soon she could excuse herself and get on with dinner preparations. Finally, she asked the expected question, "Could you stay and have dinner with us?"

The preacher always graciously accepted and said, "I'll just step outside and meet your husband when he comes in from the field."

This time, no special preparation could be made. The preacher had to take potluck, but as he slicked up his plate with a corner of Mother's homemade yeast bread, he always said it was the best meal he had tasted in days.

Sadly, times have changed and a minister can no longer maintain a firm visiting schedule. Inviting the preacher to a home-cooked meal is about as obsolete as the 5-cent ice-cream cone.

Maybe the Good Old Days weren't better, but when it comes to getting acquainted, there's nothing like a homey meal around the kitchen table. Mother knew how to welcome her pastors. She invited them to dinner! ❖

Sermon With a Haircut

By Barbara Barton

On Sunday morning, you could hear a sermon and get a haircut on our front porch, all at the same time. We lived on a knoll just above the swamps of Franklin Parish, La., in the 1920s. Our farm was near enough to the water that we could almost hear the alligators flapping their tails.

As you came up the hill from the swamp, you could see our house in a clearing with fields nearby. It was a weathered wooden structure with a long front porch running the length of the house. No foundation was under it. Instead, the house sat on large rocks that left plenty of room underneath for the chickens and small pigs to roam. I guess it was what you called a "high-water" house.

Sharecropping a cotton farm kept my family pretty busy six days a week. Dad plowed with a team of horses or mules, and we kids hoed the cotton. My dad was also a pretty good barber, but as a farmer, he didn't have any free time to give the neighbors a haircut until Sunday morning. When the Sabbath dawned, the snipping began.

Early on that day, Dad would put his chair outside on our large, sprawling porch, sharpen his scissors and open his barbershop. Our neighbors began to come, one or two at a time, from around those big, moss-filled cypress trees. Some came by boat, and we could hear them banging their guidepoles to bring their boats near the landing.

They knew us well. Our house was near the landing in the swamp where they paddled their boats out of the alligator-infested water and came ashore. On weekdays, some of the swamp-dwellers would borrow our wagon and team to got into town for supplies. When they returned, we'd visit and put up the mules. They'd load their parcels in the boats and glide silently into the swamp on their way home.

So as each Sabbath day began, we looked for friends to come. The gathering included a combination of black people and whites, so it wasn't unusual that a black preacher heard about the small group meeting every Sunday at our house. He thought it would be a good place to sound out the Word of God.

He figured "where two or three are gathered" afforded him a captive audience. The preacher expounded on the Word of God, and we had receptive ears. Here was the scene: Dad snipping hair on one end of the porch while this man of God sang and extolled the Gospel from the other end. Eight or 10 people would usually gather around the preacher to listen.

If Dad finished cutting hair early, he would bring out his fiddle to play along with the hymns. It wasn't until I was older that I realized that fiddle—I mean that violin—was pretty special. He called it a Stradivarius.

How we owned such an instrument, I'll never know. After all, we were sharecroppers who didn't even own our land. Whether the fiddle was a copy of the real thing doesn't matter. It made the sweetest music. Dad was also known to fire it up at dances on other occasions.

My mother was sickly and usually reclined on a bed just inside the house. There she raised the window enough to hear strains of *Amazing Grace* and the preacher's fire-and-brimstone messages.

I learned to cook at an early age since she was bedridden. Sometimes we had made teacakes and invited the little crowd for cakes and coffee on the porch before they left. I couldn't invite them into our living room because we didn't have one. In Louisiana, though, you always had coffee brewing in the middle of the morning. The rest of the world may think Louisiana coffee is strong, but we thought it hit the spot.

Dad never charged for the haircuts, but we were well paid by those families who cared for us. I was taught to cook by an elderly neighbor who knew I needed help.

Franklin Parish is a pleasant memory as I think about the friends we had and how people loved one another. Life had simpler needs and simpler ways. ❖

Circuit-Riding Preacher

By Arthur Williams

any years ago, I made a trip to the place where I was born. I don't know what made me decide to go, it having been years since I'd left the place. The only reason I can figure is I must have been just a mite lonesome.

When people reach the later years in their lives, they seem to let their minds wander back over the paths they have traveled. They like to review the things they have done, the things they didn't do that they should have done, and the things that might have been, but never happened.

I'd left this community when I was 10 years old, in 1906. I'd never been back, even though for a number of years, I'd lived only 12 miles away in a rip-roaring logging camp.

When I left this old home of mine, there were no roads except those made by the natives so they could drive their horses, mules or oxen to Buna, 12 miles away, for supplies. It took from sun to sun to make the trip to and from Buna.

> **When I left this old home of mine, there were no roads except those made by the natives so they could drive their horses, mules or oxen.**

What a difference—a paved, concrete, all-weather road reached our very door. Just before I got to our old home, I saw the church, sitting in the same place it used to be. Of course, it had been remodeled from time to time, but it had had a fresh coat of paint recently and it looked as good as it did the day I left. I stopped, looked at the old church for a while, then I drove on toward our old house. As I drove, memories flashed through my mind.

I drove up in front of the old home. I was surprised to see it looking almost like it did the day I left. A man came out to the front gate to meet me. I told him who I was, and that I'd like to look around for old times' sake. He asked me into the house. We had a cup of coffee, and while we drank it, my eyes wandered to every nook and corner.

I was sitting right in the spot where my mother's bed was when she gave birth to me. I could reach down from my chair and touch the very spot. Just the thought of being so near made cold chills run up and down my spine.

Many memories of events and places I hadn't recalled in years came back as plain as if they had happened yesterday. One of the most vivid memories was of the old church I'd passed on the way in. It was where I saw my father and mother join the Baptist church. It was where we worshipped for as long as we lived here. Being both church and school, it was also the place where I'd spent my first days in school. But what stood out more vividly were the times we went to church on Saturday night, Sunday and Sunday night.

We didn't have a regular preacher like most churches do nowadays. We usually had a circuit rider who made it to our church about every six weeks. He would come in early and be ready to preach Saturday night, Sunday and Sunday night. He would stay with some of the church members so he had room and board for himself and his horse.

I was only about 4 years old at the time, but I remember so well when the preacher stayed at our house. It always meant chicken, fried to a crispy brown, and cream gravy and plenty of buttermilk biscuits, not the one-bite size, but about the size of the average saucer. I can see my mother now, as she patted that biscuit dough from one hand to the other, forming those large buttermilk biscuits for cooking in the old wood-burning cast-iron cookstove.

They would ask the preacher to say grace. Then the large platter of golden-brown chicken would be passed to the preacher first. I've always heard it was the Methodists who were so hard on fried chicken, but if there is anyone from any denomination who could top this old backwoods Baptist, I would sure like to see him.

Everybody went to church, especially on Sunday. Mama would get everything ready to cook before she left, so there would be no lost time getting dinner on the table once we were home from church.

A number of years ago I heard a preacher say, "Don't send your children to church or Sunday school—take them." That is just what Mama and Dad did. They took my brother and me to church, and they saw that we behaved while we were there.

Our church didn't have any piano, organ or any kind of music, but they had some singers,

Finally, when the preacher became so hoarse he could hardly talk, the choir would sing Amazing Grace *and* Rock of Ages.

and even though they might not have sung too well, they sure did sing loud.

After singing a couple of songs, the preacher would pray. Sometimes he would get carried away and the prayer would be rather long. After the prayer, he would start his sermon. When he started, he would be wearing a coat, collar and tie, but when he finished, he looked like he had been run through a cotton gin.

He would start off kinda slow, maybe telling about some of his experiences on the circuit. Then he would read his text for the day, and he was on his way.

This preacher hadn't prepared any sermon. He didn't have anything written down; what he said just flowed right out from the heart. When he started getting warm, there being no fans or air conditioning in those days, he would take off his coat. Then, as he worked further into his discourse, he would unbutton his collar and take off his necktie.

By this time, he was into the fire-and-brimstone part of his sermon. His hair was down in his eyes, the sweat pouring down his face. Then he got to talking about that bottomless pit of fire and brimstone, where the unbelievers and the unbaptized would burn forever and ever. Even though I was only 4 years old, cold sweat popped out all over my body. I was so dad-blamed scared—until I slipped over close to my mother and hid my head under her arm. From then on, I watched and listened to the preacher with one eye peeking out.

Finally, when the preacher became so hoarse he could hardly talk, he would end his sermon by opening the doors of the church. The choir would sing *Amazing Grace* and *Rock of Ages*, and the preacher would come down from the platform and plead with his listeners to come on and give their lives to God. Then he would tell them where they would end up if they kept holding back. "You," he told them, "will end up right in the bottom of that pit of fire of everlasting brimstone which is the hottest fire there is or ever will be!"

"You know how it hurts when you burn your finger on a red-hot stove!" he said. "Well, let me tell

you right here and now," and he pointed his finger at them as he walked up and down in front of them like a caged lion, "you don't know what the new day brings forth! This may be your last chance to repent and give your life to God! If you should be taken away before you have another chance, think—just think where you would end up!"

Then he would talk soft and low: "When you are suffering the torture of the damned for all eternity, don't you yell out and blame me for your trouble. Don't cry out in your pain and say you didn't know. Don't cry out to the Lord and say you didn't have a chance, for the Lord knows I gave you that chance this very night. This very moment, as we are assembled here and I am pleading with you to make just a few short steps and be saved, is recorded in the Lord's book in His heavenly home. The Lord knows everything—and don't you ever forget that."

The preacher would ask the choir to sing a few more verses, and while they were singing, he would give the congregation one last chance to escape hellfire and damnation. Then someone whom the preacher had scared the living daylights out of would come forward. The preacher would yell out, "Praise the Lord for guiding this poor lost soul toward a heavenly home!"

After church, we drove the 3 miles home. I always sat in the back of the wagon with my feet hanging down.

When Mama finally got dinner on the table, and the preacher had asked the blessing, you never did see anybody jump into that fried chicken, buttermilk biscuits and cream gravy like that preacher did. I was always the last to be served. By the time the chicken got to me, my favorite pieces were gone. I just had to take the leavings. Anyway, there was always the peach cobbler and "sweet tater" pie.

For a few weeks after one of these hellfire-and-brimstone sermons, I was almost an angel. If I happened to get out of line, all Mama had to do was remind me where all the bad boys ended up, and I straightened up at once.

I tried my level best to be a good boy and do like the preacher said, but to be real truthful with you, I think maybe I had a little envy in my heart against that preacher, when Papa passed the chicken and he took my pulley bone. ❖

How Parson Williams Broke the Sabbath

On the grave of Parson Williams,
the grass is dry and bleached.
It is more than 50 winters,
since he lived and laughed and preached.
But his mem'ry in New England
no winter snow can kill.
Of his goodness and his drollness,
countless legends linger still.
And among these treasured legends,
I hold this one as a boon—
How he got in Deacon Crosby's hay
on a Sunday afternoon.
He was midway in a sermon,
most orthodox, on grace,
When a sound of distant thunder
broke the quiet of the place.
Now the meadow of the Crosbys
lay full within his sight,
As he glanced from out the window
that stood open on his right.
And the green and fragrant haycocks
by acres there did stand,
Not a meadow like the deacon's
far or near in all the land.
Quick and loud the claps of thunder
went rolling to the skies,

And the parson saw his deacon
looking out with anxious eyes.
"Now, my brethren," called the parson,
and he called with might and main,
"We must get in Brother Crosby's hay:
'Tis our duty now most plain."
And he shut the great red Bible
and tossed his sermon down;
Not a man could turn more swiftly
than the parson in that town,
And he ran now to the meadow,
with all his strength and speed,
And the congregation followed,
all bewildered in his lead.
With a will they worked and shouted,
and cleared the fields apace;
And the parson led the singing
while the sweat rolled down his face,
And it thundered louder,
and dark grew east and west,
But the hay was under cover,
and the parson had worked best.
And again in pew and pulpit,
their places took, composed,
And the parson preached his sermon,
to "fifteenth" where it closed.
—*Anonymous*

Wheatland

By Marion Shoeberlein

Whenever I saw my grandmother's house in Wheatland, the country parsonage did not impress me at all. From the outside it looked like any other country house, only it needed a coat of paint a little more. The moo of cows, though, and the neigh of the horses was something to hear, as I came from a city of coughing automobiles and buses.

The saddest summer was the one after Grandfather died and we went there to bring Grandmother home with us for good. I was 13 years old, and Wheatland had come to mean a great deal more to me.

Grandmother made several trips to the cemetery in back of the church before she left. Grandfather and an infant son were buried there. As she stood there with all the June grass and trees around her, I imagined her whole life passed before her eyes. This was the closing chapter of the book.

"Grandmother," was all I could say. I couldn't tell her to forget or whisper any words of comfort. I was too young.

All that week the farm people who had been Grandfather's church members came to bid her goodbye. They brought her little presents of canned goods and aprons and towels. They brought her wishes and smiles and tears.

As we got into the automobile that would take us home to Chicago, I tried to go back in my mind a little bit with Grandmother. It was easy.

I had vivid recollections of Grandfather preaching sermons to his congregation of 100 farm people. His smile and all the personality that echoed from his big voice made them feel good. He was a "fisher of men" and they had been caught. He had lived in Wheatland for the last 20 years of his life, and Grandmother had always said they had been his best years.

Because I was more worldly minded as a child, I did not particularly enjoy a Christmas in the country. Christmas at Wheatland was something that had to grow on you. Its beauty had to kind of "sink in." My mother and father understood that kind of beauty.

On the Sunday before Christmas, my grandfather and two or three of his strongest male parishioners would go into the woods to get the tree for the church. I never went with them because Mother said it was dangerous and the tree might fall on me. But I liked it when I heard them half-pulling and half-carrying it home, singing Christmas carols at the top of their voices.

I didn't get many presents from Grandfather and Grandmother because they didn't have the money to spend. Country preachers in those days didn't make much of a salary. I remember, though, the most beautiful present they ever gave me. It was a set of doll dishes. There were four little plates and four little cups and saucers. Each plate, saucer and cup had the Three Wise Men riding their camels painted on it. I played very carefully with them once a year at Christmastime when I gave a tea party for my dolls. The rest of the time they were locked up in my mother's china cabinet.

The Christmas Eve service at Wheatland was something to remember. All the farmers came with their children, their deep summer tans finally withered. How the farm children looked forward to getting a few apples and oranges along with a storybook in the Christmas bags at church! Their parents looked forward to hearing them say a "piece" and singing the carols.

Looking back, I realize that Wheatland wasn't just a place to my grandparents. It was a whole way of life. It was teaching sunburned farmers how to pray and marrying wild lads to gentle lassies. It was taking blueberries to sick people and singing lullabies to newborn babies. It was the milk and honey of life. The memories of all Grandmother had sown and grown during her lifetime were all she had left after Grandfather died. What more could any woman want? ❖

The Pastor's Lemonade

By Lynne Stewart

Our pastor, a widower in his 60s, always had Sunday dinner at the home of a member of his flock. Our church was small, and during the Depression, many of the church members couldn't afford to have even one extra person at the dining table, so Pastor Taylor ate with us often.

Living on a farm, we always had food, even when money was hard to come by. We referred to the day when the pastor came to dinner as "the pastor's Sunday."

Entertaining the pastor was high on Grandma's list of social events, but she seemed to think that he came to the house not only to have Sunday dinner with us, but also to see if he could find a speck of dust in some dark corner and to inspect the house for evidence of sin. The house had to be spotless, stainless, neat and, ideally, germ-free.

Sheet music was removed form the piano and replaced with a hymnal. All the movie magazines were hidden away because Grandma didn't know if Pastor Taylor approved of motion pictures. She hid our deck of cards because she was sure he frowned on gambling, even when betting was done with nothing more than matchsticks.

I went into the dining room, thinking about the amount of lemonade the pastor had consumed and, to my chagrin, I asked, "Pastor Brownlee, do you want four more glasses of lemonade?"

Her bottles of dandelion wine that she made and used for medicinal purposes were pushed back into a corner of the pantry lest the pastor notice one and suspect her of taking an occasional nip.

For a couple of days before the pastor's Sunday, we cleaned house. The house was scrubbed and polished from front to back, side to side and top to bottom.

My brothers made up the rug-beating brigade. After rolling up the living-room and dining-room rugs and carrying them outside, they hung them across the clothesline and gave them an unmerciful pounding with wire rug beaters.

My older sisters, Barbara and Jeanne, were the window washers. Joyce and I, armed with dusting cloths, battled any dust that had settled in the house. Grandma acted as first sergeant, checking first on one group of workers, then another.

On Sunday morning, Grandma and the older girls were up early baking and cooking. The best dishes and the linen tablecloth were brought out for the pastor's Sunday. We were all told to be on our best behavior, mind our table manners and speak only when we were spoken to. By the time the pastor arrived, we were all nervous wrecks.

In time, Pastor Taylor's failing health forced him to bid his flock goodbye. He was replaced by Pastor Brownlee, a young, single, good-natured man who set Jeanne's heart aflutter. Jeanne was 20 years old with no engagement ring on her finger and not even a steady boyfriend. Soon, she and the new pastor were seeing each other socially.

During the week before Pastor Brownlee's first visit, Grandma gave us the usual lectures about being on our best behavior—and this time Jeanne got in on the act.

She lectured us more often than Grandma did and made it clear that we would be truly sorry if we did or said anything to embarrass her in front of Pastor Brownlee. She also made us work twice as hard cleaning the house. We scrubbed, dusted and polished until we were sure there would be no varnish left on the furniture.

During Pastor Brownlee's first Sunday dinner with us, everything went smoothly until after we had finished our dessert. While Dad, Uncle Tony, Jeanne and Barbara remained at the table with the pastor, Grandma began clearing the dishes away and tidying up the kitchen. Joyce and I joined her.

"One of you go ask the pastor if he wants another glass of lemonade," Grandma said.

"He won't want any more," I said. "He's already had four."

"It's hot today, so cold drinks taste good. Go ask him if he wants more," she ordered.

"After four, he couldn't hold any more," I insisted.

During the argument that followed, the pastor's four glasses of lemonade were hashed over to the point that they were the only things on my mind.

"Do as you're told!" Grandma snapped. "Go in there and ask if he wants more lemonade."

I went into the dining room, thinking about the amount of lemonade the pastor had consumed and, to my chagrin, I asked, "Pastor Brownlee, do you want four more glasses of lemonade?"

I didn't find out if he wanted even one more glass, because realizing what I had said, I ran upstairs and stayed there until the pastor left the house. For the next week, Jeanne frequently told me that if the pastor dropped her like a hot potato, it would be my fault.

Grandma assured me that if my sister met the fate of a hot potato it would have nothing to do with me, but I worried about it until the day when Jeanne became Mrs. Brownlee. ❖

The Preacher's No Fool!

By Marie Cole Colasuonno

Ironically, the rowdy frontier town of Mobridge, S.D., was slated to be my gentle, scholarly father's first parish following his graduation from Oberlin Seminary.

In 1910, Mobridge was a rugged railroad division-point town, not far removed from homesteading days. It must have been a challenge for a bookish minister from New Hampshire to fit in with the local townsfolk, but Dad worked at it.

All the young bachelors took their meals together at the same restaurant, and Dad became well acquainted with them in short order. He had red hair and a dry wit, and he soon convinced even the most skeptical of the young locals that the new preacher was all right.

The Mobridge Congregational Church was in its infancy, and it was Dad's mission to build one, both literally and figuratively. He not only had to raise funds for the physical structure, but also cast about for members and Sunday-school teachers.

Dad always called shivarees a "barbaric custom," so when he got wind of this scheme, he quietly set about thwarting it.

Someone suggested that Cap'n Jacobsen's daughter, the new schoolteacher, might be interested in helping out so Dad went out one April day to talk to her.

Apparently, when he met the vivacious, glowing Miss Jacobsen, he forgot all about his search for a Sunday-school teacher. She fed him burned birthday cake—and he was enchanted. The courtship was on: an old-fashioned country courtship. For example, they went a-Maying on May Day to pick wild roses. By the end of June, to no one's surprise, they had set their wedding date for October.

Meanwhile, Dad had a church to build and dedicate before his wedding rolled around. It must have taken a good bit of New England discipline to concentrate on his job instead of his fiancée, but he persevered, and the church was dedicated the Sunday before they were to be married.

In the meantime, his rowdy bachelor cronies were plotting a "shivaree," a rural tradition that involved disrupting the honeymoon. The preacher's wedding seemed a prime opportunity for such an event. Since many of the town's bachelors were not inclined to set foot inside a

church for any reason, they wouldn't be at the wedding, but they did arrange to have a confederate stationed there to ring the church bell as soon as the ceremony was over.

They planned to seize the bride on the church steps, transport her down into the middle of town and seat her on a throne of beer kegs, while the unfortunate groom would be abducted and taken far, far out of town, and left to walk back.

Dad always called shivarees a "barbaric custom," so when he got wind of this scheme, he quietly set about thwarting it. The day before the wedding, he and Mother quietly slipped into the church, climbed up in the belfry, and tied the bell rope to a nearby rafter.

Meanwhile, he had written a note to the division superintendent of the railroad to ask whether the train could make an unscheduled stop a quarter-mile down the track past the Mobridge station. Also, he enlisted the aid of Mother's brother, Henry. His tasks were to see that their luggage got on the train at the station, and to keep them abreast of the plans in town.

On the day of the wedding, the church filled with wedding guests and the ceremony was duly performed. The couple filed decorously down the aisle afterward, but the minute they were out the church door, they made a run for it. Meanwhile,

the inside conspirator fruitless tugged at the church bell, which was strangely silent.

Uncle Henry was able to drive them unperceived down to the crossing a quarter-mile out of town. They stood there, shivering in the dark and listening to the raucous shouts of the crowd milling around in frustration at the station. When Uncle Henry later appeared at the station, bland and innocent, with the couple's luggage, they peppered him with queries: "Where is the preacher, Henry?" He disclaimed any knowledge and said all he knew was that he was to load their luggage onto the incoming train.

Meantime, Mother and Dad still didn't know whether the division superintendent had gotten their letter and, even if he had, whether he would grant such a frivolous request. They were standing there in the dusk, waiting, when all of a sudden someone approached and said, "That you, Cole?"

"Yes," said Dad. And there was that dear division superintendent of the railroad, who had come down in person to see that the train stopped to pick them up. And it did.

The next day Mother and Dad sent a message back to the disappointed plotters, and it was posted in the bank window: "Having a wonderful time. Feed the rice to the chickens." ❖

Mountain Religion

By Charles B. O'Dooley

People in the hills of West Virginia, where I was born and raised up, tend to take their religion very seriously. They were a Godfearing, down-to-earth people who worshiped like they worked: hard and diligently. When they talked to God, they believed that He heard them and expected action. As one old mountaineer put it in a prayer, "Lord, I'm not asking for a faith that would move yonder mountain. I can take enough dynamite and move it, if it needs movin'. I pray, Lord, for enough faith to move me."

We had a church on the Old Kingwood Pike that was called Hog Back Church. It was nicknamed that because it sat up on posts and hogs went under it to get out of the sun and slept there at night. Sometimes during a service, they would rub their backs against the floor beams and grunt and carry on.

One summer while a revival meeting was going on, a visitor from the city came to visit one of the local families. They took him to church that night. The preacher was preaching on the eighth chapter of Luke, in which Jesus commands some evil spirits to come out of a man; the demons entered a herd of swine the man was tending and ran into the lake and drowned.

They were all standing there when they saw a little girl about 9 years old coming down the road with an umbrella under her arm.

Now, mountain preachers get really worked up when they preach. They preach in a loud voice, use their hands and sometimes stomp their feet to bring across a point. Well, just as the preacher said that Jesus sent the spirits into the swine, he stomped his foot good and hard on the floor and woke the hogs that were sleeping under the church. Well sir, when the city visitor heard them, he turned white as a ghost and shook all over! We later heard that when he went back to the city, he told his friend that there was a preacher in them hills who could preach a sermon so real that he could actually hear the hogs that were mentioned in the message!

This was back around 1932, and times were really hard; it kept a man humping just to feed his family. One man had a large family and nothing in the larder to feed them. That night at church, he prayed, "Oh Lord, you know that I have nine children and I can't find no work, and, Lord, them children are hungry. You say in Your Word that if we ask, we will receive, so, Lord, I'm asking You to send me a barrel of flour; Lord, send me a barrel of sugar; Lord, send me a barrel of molasses; Lord, send me a barrel of salt; Lord, send me a barrel of pepper—hold on, Lord, that's too darn much pepper."

The Brown family lived on the mountain next to the church. They were great singers, and on a clear evening, you could hear them singing for miles. Three brothers in the large family attended church regularly and really took their religion to heart. I was at the country store one day when a man was telling how he was squirrel hunting when he had come across the older brother, Willey, praying loudly at the bottom of a cliff: "God, I have told you all the things I have been doing for you, and if you think I'm lying, then I hope that this cliff will fall upon me."

The man said he rolled some small rocks over the edge of the cliff. They landed right beside Willey's feet, and Willey said, "Lord, can't you take a joke?"

I saw many strange occurrences at Hog Back Church, but they still talk about one that we boys kind of helped along. The church didn't have a regular preacher at the time, and one of the members took over to act as a lay preacher 'til a regular one came along. It was getting on toward winter and there was hardly any coal to build fires in the big Burningside stove that heated the church.

The lay preacher (we'll call him Brother Joe) informed the congregation of this fact, but his announcement failed to produce enough money in the collection plate to purchase sufficient coal to last through the winter. We could see the cold, sour expression on Joe's face, and we all knew that the sermon the following Sunday night would be one of his famous fire-and-brimstone addresses.

When Brother Joe preached, he didn't just stand behind the pulpit, but walked up and down the aisle, back and forth in front of the pulpit. When Joe walked, he shuffled his feet on the hard pine floor, and knowing this, we boys decided to help him put his fire-and-brimstone sermon across. We got two boxes of farmer matches and took the heads off of them. Then we ground them into a fine powder and sprinkled it on the floor where Joe would be shuffling up and down.

Now, anybody knows that match heads are made mainly of sulfur; with a little friction (such as Joe's shoes rubbing it against the floor), it will produce sparks, a little smoke and a smell like brimstone. When Brother Joe preached his fire-and-brimstone sermon the next Sunday night, he made quite an impression. As he shuffled across the floor, the congregation could see the smoke and smell the brimstone. It resulted in a large collection, more than enough to buy coal for the winter!

I mentioned before the deep and sincere faith that mountain people have. In the summer of 1930, we had a dry spell that lasted for some time. The river at Morgantown, W.Va., had gotten so low that only a small stream ran down the middle of the riverbed. We had a new preacher at Hog Back Church by then, and he announced at the regular Wednesday prayer meeting that he wanted everyone to come the next day to pray for rain. The next day, the preacher was standing on the steps to welcome the people as they came in. As it was real hot that day, the people were standing outside to wait until everyone got there before going in.

They were all standing there when they saw a little girl about 9 years old coming down the road with an umbrella under her arm. When she got to the steps, the new preacher said to her, "Why, little girl, what in the world are you carrying an umbrella for?"

She said, "We came to pray for rain, didn't we?"

I don't know if the praying had anything to do with it or not, but that night a soft, quiet rain came and lasted all night and broke the drought. ❖

Billy Sunday: The Sawdust Trail

By Duane Valentry

The small midwestern town had never known such excitement. Churches for miles around had united to bring Billy Sunday, greatest speaker of his day, to the community. No man, woman or child would miss seeing and hearing the fiery evangelist.

The name "Billy Sunday" was probably mentioned every day in every house. The newspapers followed his travels with banner headlines. The colorful ex-baseball star, almost a legend in his time, had only to make an appearance and people from hundreds of miles around would drop everything to come to hear him.

It is doubtful that any individual in modern times did as much as Billy Sunday did to help the cause of temperance. He caught the imagination of America as few men ever have. His vivid sermons on the evil of drink made converts by the tens of thousands and roused people to vote the saloon, then the symbol of the liquor traffic, out of existence.

But no group could stop the mouth of this man whose phrases were repeated all over the country.

"The saloon is the sum of all villainies," he preached. "It is worse than war or pestilence. It is the crime of crimes, the appalling source of slavery, poverty and sorrow!"

Far from turning off listeners, his language mesmerized his hearers, although (as may be imagined) it did not endear him to the liquor industry. There was quick retaliation.

"The liquor people seem to know of his engagements as soon as he makes them, and weeks ahead of his meetings they begin to circulate all manner of lying slanders against him," said one of Sunday's associates. "It is well authenticated that they spend thousands yearly doing this."

But no group could stop the mouth of this man whose phrases were repeated all over the country. The forthright, down-to-earth Billy appealed to men of all ages and callings.

At 21, the popular evangelist (who had been born in a log cabin in Iowa and raised in an orphanage) was discovered by Pop Anson of the Chicago White Stockings while playing a spectacular game for the city baseball team in Marshalltown. Anson persuaded the boy his calling lay with the major leagues and thus Billy was one of the few ever to go from the "prairie" to the big time in one stride. Always a fast runner, his speed gave him an edge over more experienced teammates, and he was soon known as the fastest man in baseball.

One day in 1886, after a night of painting the town, Billy and his friends lingered on a Chicago street to hear some Gospel singers pump an organ and sing hymns. Listening, Billy sat down on the curb with his head in his hands, unashamedly crying, for these were the hymns of his boyhood that his mother had sung.

"Boys, I'm through!" he told his friends. They laughed, but he meant it. Invited to the Pacific Garden Mission, Billy became a frequent visitor and was soon converted to active Christianity. A job at the YMCA began to absorb his spare time. He threw all his amazing energy into the work.

The newly converted baseball star bought a secondhand Bible for 35 cents. He joined the Presbyterian Church and taught Sunday school. Boys, he soon found, wanted to talk baseball, but he countered this by promising to tell them all they wanted to know about the game any other day of the week—but Sunday belonged to God.

Speaking to youth groups and churches, Sunday soon showed promise of the eloquence that would make him famous. He also resented the chains that bound him to baseball. He now had more of a heart for religious activity, but his contract had several more years and he was valuable to his team.

"After he became a Christian, his managers seemed to be even more anxious to keep him, on account of his good influence over other players," said a teammate. "Every man of them had a higher respect for him for the stand he took, and cut out profanity and rough talk when with him."

Wanting out of the game, Billy prayed. No one knew better than he did that a contract is a contract, yet he felt his calling lay elsewhere. Then occurred one of those events skeptics would not call an answer to prayer, but which nonetheless released Sunday for the work he wanted to do. Many old National League players had withdrawn from their teams to establish the Brotherhood Association, forerunner of the American League. But in 1891, these men returned to the National League, so flooding the baseball market that his

managers were willing to let him go. Thus ended the sports career of a great star whose goal in life would now be the saving of souls.

Billy Sunday is said to have preached to 80 million men, women and children —before the days of radio and television, an astounding total. In 35 years of successful preaching, he converted a million people and was the greatest single power responsible for Prohibition.

Sunday preached with a fury few have equaled before or since. So fervent was his speech and so vigorous his style that he found it necessary to carry a physical trainer with him on tour. Yet he never tired.

In the height of his popularity, Sunday campaigns were held in temporary wooden buildings, or tabernacles. The tabernacle floor was covered with sawdust. "The sawdust trail"— a phrase synonymous with firebrand traveling evangelism—was coined when a newly converted soul made the walk up those aisles to shake Sunday's hand after accepting the call of Christ.

Many criticized Sunday; more were his admirers. During his visit to New York in 1917, he preached to 1.25 million and converted 100,000. His sermons against liquor were soon famous across the nation and turned tens of thousands into abstainers, as he fought to close saloons—and did, especially where he preached.

Today there are no "booze battlers" like the one and only Billy Sunday—a David not afraid to cast stones without ceasing at a Goliath who is now more powerful than ever. Were he here, he would surely be in the forefront of battle, as always! ❖

Pioneer Preacher

By Eleanore Bopp Peterson

As a young family in the early '1930s, we lived in a flat owned by my grandparents in Milwaukee. There were two of us kids, my brother, Alden, then age 2, and me, age 6. Dad had a steady job as chauffeur for a wealthy widow and we were doing quite well compared to other families at that time.

Dad developed a strange inward restlessness, however, and one day confided to Mom, "Marie, I feel God wants me in the ministry!" Mom was not surprised. She had sensed his preoccupation and felt, too, that God had other plans for them. She suggested that he discuss this with our pastor, who counseled him.

In good times, the ministry was not an easy life, and surely now the Depression demanded even greater sacrifice, so Mom and Dad prayed for guidance.

Now, in those early days of our denomination, there were no seminaries. Young men who had a call to the ministry studied on their own and learned from the advice and experiences of older preachers. For months, Dad studied the Bible and books on doctrine and pastoral ethics with the help of our pastor. Dad wanted to be prepared.

Months went by, however, and nothing unusual happened. At times, I'm sure, doubts filled his mind. Had he made a mistake? But then one day Dad came home with news that initiated a drastic turn of events.

"Roy," his employer had said, "I'm planning to leave for Europe. I won't need your services any longer." Dad was without a job! Now to most young couples such news would be devastating, but my parents were neither depressed nor upset. They saw this as an answer to their prayers. God had closed one door, and they knew He would open another.

Shortly after his layoff, Dad learned from a pastor-friend that a pastor from a neighboring town had held nightly revival meetings for three weeks and now needed someone to succeed him since he had obligations to his own congregation. My parents were introduced to this pastor, and, in due time, Dad was asked to shepherd the small flock. This invitation confirmed God's call upon their lives, so when the arrangements were made, Mom and Dad packed their belongings in a trailer, chucked us kids in the loaded Model A and headed for their mission field.

Mom had carefully saved $82 hidden between the cushions of the davenport for just such a time. That meager nest egg became our sole support.

Consequently, the neophyte congregation needed a place to worship, but building during the Depression was impossible. However, there was an old vacated feed store on Main Street. The owners gladly agreed to rent it for $9 per month if we cleaned it up. The next few weeks were

My parents were introduced to this pastor, and, in due time, Dad was asked to shepherd the small flock.

busy ones. The women enthusiastically scrubbed, painted and papered the store and adjacent living quarters, which would be the parsonage. Dad and the men built a pine pulpit and benches and set up an old potbellied stove. Dad hauled an old upright piano from Milwaukee on a trailer behind his Ford. Finally, they painted the front display windows for privacy and hung up a sign outside—"Ontario Gospel Tabernacle."

There it was, finished. Only a storefront church, but the pride of hardworking, resourceful, God-fearing people! It was to be a place of comfort and reassurance during dark, days ahead. But, for me, it was a traumatic time. Being a shy little girl, adapting to a new home and school was difficult. In the evenings, I'd often sit in the swing Dad made for us in the big cedar tree and think about my girlfriend in Milwaukee. Tears of lonesomeness trickled down my cheeks more than once.

The economy of the country at that time was at an all-time low. Many people were jobless, except for those who worked in the Civilian Conservation Corps or on other government projects, so it was not unusual to often have less than 50 cents in the offering basket on Sundays. But somehow, by the time the rent was due, there was always enough saved—except for one time.

The giving had been especially poor that month and Dad wondered how he could pay the rent. Would they lose the building they had all worked so hard for? He and Mom prayed for God to meet this need. A few days later Dad went to the post office to get mail and came home with two letters from friends. Tucked inside of one was $4 and a $5 bill fell out of the other! Just enough for the rent. It was a direct answer to prayer.

Although money was scarce, we never went hungry. We had a large garden and Mom did a lot of canning and baking. There was a wonderful spirit of sharing in those days, too. Once a month, the congregation had a "pound party." Each family brought baked goods, canned foods, dried prunes, rice, or whatever, and set them on the platform for us. I remember how exciting it was to open all the goodies in the parsonage after the service and unpack them.

Every community has its colorful characters. Idie and Jake were an elderly couple who lived in a tar-paper shack on the edge of town. Jake was a tall, gaunt Norwegian. Leathery skin stretched tautly across his log, bony nose and high cheekbones, and a scraggly beard stained with tobacco gave him the appearance of a would-be Viking. He was a quiet, passive fellow, though.

Idie was short and plump. Her gray, wiry hair gave her a frowsy appearance. Unlike Jake, Idie was feisty. Stories circulated that once someone had accidentally stepped on her skirt that dragged behind her and she cursed him in no uncertain terms. Some claimed she carried a knife in the folds of her skirt. But, in spite of their reputation, they were faithful church attenders. Idie would come early, kick off her shoes and sit barefooted during the services. She and Jake usually sat near the back. Underneath all of this, they were two lonely souls who yearned for acceptance.

One Sunday, Jake came to our house with his wheelbarrow piled high with squash and potatoes. After the service, Dad said to Okey John, "Say, Idie and Jake sure know how to raise beautiful potatoes!" Okey John, who was their neighbor, smiled wryly.

"No, Preacher. Them taters are mine. Last night I saw Idie digging them up with her hands and stuffing the tops back in so no one would know!" (That time the sharing idea backfired. There was still a lot of teaching and preaching that needed to be done.)

For many years, my parents made an annual trek to visit their "old stomping grounds." They reminisced as they drove through town or stopped to talk with an old-timer, sitting on a bench outside the general store. I've often heard them say that first year in the ministry was the happiest and richest of their entire lives. The finest seminary could never duplicate the lessons they learned from ministering to those simple folk in the small Wisconsin community.

Dad was later ordained by the Assemblies of God. He was in active ministry for 35 years and served five churches successfully. Dad has passed on to his reward now, but the experience he and Mom had during his first year in the ministry exemplifies true pioneer spirit. ❖

Revivals, Socials & Goin' to Meetin'

Chapter Three

*I*s it just me, or does it seem that we spend more time these days with cars, televisions and computers than with people? It wasn't always like that. In the Good Old Days recreation, leisure, plus all things spiritual revolved around getting together with other folks. Looking back, if it weren't for school and church this farm kid would have had no social life at all.

Revivals, socials and "goin' to meetin' " were the ticket to much more than just contact with God.

How many of us first braved the foray toward the opposite sex at some church event? First contact was a smile, then a shy chat, maybe a shared pew at a prayer meeting—pretty soon you found yourself bidding on her box at the next social.

Besides seeking God, neighbors sought each other at those gatherings. Ladies sought a pickle recipe or help with a colicky baby. Men sought advice on crops or help with a team of mules. Children just sought other children for marble shooting, rope jumping, tag playing fun.

Then there was the entertainment factor.

My best friend Chet and I once made our way to a charismatic tent revival, sitting about halfway down the sawdust trail and drinking in the evening's festivities mainly because there was little else to do within a couple of miles of our homes. Chet was about 12 and I was 11 on that sweltering summer evening long ago, and we had never been to a "holy roller" revival. Oh, my own Pentecostal church had its share of people who would be touched by the Spirit, but I had never witnessed a full-blown episode of tongue-speaking, soul-moaning, aisle-filling holy rolling before.

The service began with the customary, obligatory hymns, prayers and Bible verses. Then the evangelist got down to business. Before we knew what had happened, a lady a couple of rows in front of us began to quake, moaning first and then babbling loudly before falling into the aisle gyrating to the beat of the Spirit. She was joined by another and another as the evangelist kept the service whipped into a high pitch.

I have been forgiven since, but the view from my pew was humorous. I began to snicker and Chet joined me. Pretty soon we were laughing hard, holding our sides and gasping for breath.

Suddenly I was struck from behind—whack!—by a woman's purse. I reckoned that some indignant Christian had grown tired of our sacrilege and was righteously punishing us in the place of God Himself. Instead, as soon as the blow had been laid, the woman's voice rang out: "Praise the Lord! These boys have got the Spirit!"

Suddenly we were the center of attention, pummeled from all sides by Spirit-filled revivalists intent on helping us live the experience to the fullest. Of course, the more they shouted, the harder we laughed and the more they praised. Chet and I rolled to the ground, adding to the frenzy. Our only escape was to crawl out of the center of attention, under the wooden benches, between legs and around the rollers to the back of the tent and into the sultry August evening.

Since those days I have come to understand a bit more about things spiritual. I know now that revivals aren't just a three-ring circus beneath the Big Top. But back in the Good Old Days revivals, socials and "goin' to meetin' " were better than any television show or video game.

—*Ken Tate*

Spring Revival Time

By Ruth Christopher

lmost everyone in our town in South Central Missouri looked forward to spring revivals—but not Mama and I. To us it meant slaving over a hot wood stove, cooking for the preachers.

It meant humping over a washtub under the shade of a big walnut tree in the back yard, washing the extra towels and bed linens as well as the clothes of the preacher and his family, which usually consisted of a wife and at least two youngsters. And then the ironing! Nobody knew about wash-and-wear back then.

Nobody else ever asked the preachers home with them because nobody else had as many bedrooms as we had. Mama didn't exactly resent keeping the preachers, but often she would be too tired to attend the services herself after cooking three meals a day and keeping the house going. And it did go against the grain with her to miss church.

But I resented this obligation! I really begrudged spending money at the grocery store for the coffee, sugar and flour we had to buy to cook for the preachers.

One thing for sure: Mama never slighted them. In fact, she went all out to prepare gourmet meals. But I felt that deep down, she must have thought it unfair for the other ladies of the church to shirk their duty and dump it all on her.

One afternoon my brother rushed into the house to tell us a revival was scheduled to start the following Saturday night.

One spring I especially resented keeping the preachers because I was 15 years old and had never in my life owned a brand-new coat. Mama had been saving all the egg and cream money she could spare to buy me the coat I had picked out in the big Sears catalog. Since there was no department store in our small town, we had to mail order everything we needed.

One afternoon my brother rushed into the house to tell us a revival was scheduled to start the following Saturday night. Mama groaned and said, "There goes your coat, Ruth. The preachers will eat it." From past experience I knew she was right.

I was doubly disappointed late Saturday afternoon when not one but two cars turned into our driveway. The preacher had a carload of helpers—musicians and altar workers. More work! More food! No more coat!

Right away I had to go to the grocery store. Even though he was a

member of the church, the owner of the only store in town did not offer us a special price or donate any groceries to help feed the preachers. But he did give little green tickets for each purchase, which were put into a drawing for a sewing machine, a set of dishes and a crisp, new $20 bill.

Mama had seen the dishes he had on display and how she wanted them! Ours were mismatched, chipped and some pieces were missing. These had pretty red roses and green leaves on the side, with soup bowls, little bread-and-butter plates, a big platter and a cute teapot that matched.

She wasn't interested in the sewing machine because she had an old treadle machine. It broke thread, skipped stitches and completely quit working at the most crucial times, but Mama knew how to get it sewing again.

This particular year the revival lasted three long weeks and we had a big stack of green tickets. I was sure we had more than anyone else in town and stood a good chance of winning the coveted dishes. I wanted them for my mother with all my heart. I thought she deserved them for keeping the preachers when no one else pitched in to relieve her.

Imagine our surprise—and disappointment—when Mama's number was called and Papa went forward to claim the sewing machine!

Everyone in town was excited the day of the drawing; Mama hopefully handed Papa our collection of green tickets. He waited with all the neighbors while the man in charge looked over the crowd, smiled and nodded, then looked at the numbers in his hand. Imagine our surprise—and disappointment—when Mama's number was called and Papa went forward to claim the sewing machine!

It never crossed our minds that we might trade with the lady who did win the dishes. Every woman in town had wanted the machine and I'm sure she would have been happy to trade.

But our Heavenly Father looks a long way into the future and sees our needs, because when He gave Mama that treadle sewing machine it proved to be the best thing that ever happened to her. When Papa passed away, she became the "widow seamstress" and she was besieged with orders to sew for others. Her prices were cheap and her work was neat and professional.

After I realized I would not be able to order the coat from the big catalog, I worked feeding and tending a batch of young fall chickens, hoping that Mama could spare enough roosters to sell and still order the coat before winter.

My father's sister lived in another state and she had four grown daughters who were either in college or already working. She often sent boxes of their cast-off clothing. That fall my aunt mailed a huge box of clothing and in it was a lovely coat with a beautiful red fox fur collar, much nicer than anything we could have ordered. How I strutted! No one else in town had a fur collar on her coat!

In late summer, the traveling circus came to town again. The entertainers had saved sewing for Mama because they remembered her fine work and affordable prices. So we got to order enough material from the big catalog for school dresses for me and shirts for my brother —all because we had not spent the money to order the coat.

Now Mama was thankful for the treadle sewing machine she had won. She did a little preaching herself when she reminded me of how it paid to sacrifice our time and labor even if it seemed we were "put upon" by others. She reminded me that God would eventually reward us in His own good time. ❖

A Little Bit of Heaven

By Ben Colp

Every July it came—to be exact, the last week of July.

We always went to the Ribstone Creek Camp meetings. That is, Mom and I went from our family. Mrs. McLuggen and her daughter, Lily, joined us.

Father and old Mac McLuggen took turns. Father would go one year and old Mac would stay home and do the chores, both his and Father's. The next year old Mac went and Father stayed.

It was a full day's drive by horse and wagon to the campgrounds.

By the time we arrived, they would already have the two big tents pitched. They were as big as circus tents. One served as the meeting tent and the other was the dining hall.

People came from miles. Some had fancy cars, while others had teams and wagons like we did. Everybody pitched a tent, for no one had heard of a recreational vehicle in those days.

By the time we arrived, they would already have the two big tents pitched. They were as big as circus tents. One served as the meeting tent and the other was the dining hall.

You didn't have to be a Christian to go to camp meeting. Fact is, you didn't even have to be religious.

You met all kinds there—the rich, the poor, the saints, the sinners and the saints-that-ain't. Everyone was welcome.

It was a great place to meet all those folks you had meant to visit over the year but hadn't.

"Well, well, Sister! It's good to see you," was a common greeting.

"Hi, Amy. And I'm glad to see you, too," some dear, saintly lady would reply, as the two hugged.

"Say, Amy, how's Robert?" the first lady would go on.

"Fine," the other giggled happily. "And you, Martha? How have you been keeping?"

"Oh, just fine. Yes, the Lord has been mighty good to me."

People came for other reasons, too. Like Chuck Gee, the cowboy who drifted in. Work was short. He had heard the meals were free. The only problem was no one wanted to play poker. Another thing: these people didn't seem too interested in his moonshine, either. Fussy people! He just put them down as a little queer, but they sure were friendly. Anyway, who could complain? The food was free.

"Hi, Brother, how are you today?" I heard a man greet another as I stood by the dining tent door.

"Why, fine, Brother," replied the short, bald-headed man. "I don't believe I know your name."

"Archie, Archie Box." Archie put forth his hand.

"Saul Stone." The bald gentleman shook hands.

"Say, Brother," Archie began, "I guess this isn't really the place, but I'm your Prairie Life Insurance Agent."

"Yeah," Saul hedged. "Well, I'm with Moose Oil." Saul edged away, but Archie followed.

"Perhaps I could explain our latest policy to you," Archie went on. "From one Christian to another, Christians ought to have life insurance. Our responsibility doesn't stop just because we've gone to heaven, you know."

"Later." The bald man turned away.

"I thought you said these religious people would be pushovers," Archie complained to a second man who came out of the dining-hall tent.

"Well, you got to admit there's a lot of people here," the second man answered.

Then there were those who came to see. Yes, they had heard what strange things these weirdos did at camp meetings. I mean, they shouted "Hallelujah!" 'til the white canvas side of the tent flapped in the breeze.

Some said they rolled on the ground and barked like coyotes. These people had come to see if it was true.

I liked camp meetings. Oh, it was crowded. Always was. There was always so much going on.

Softball games were on the diamond back of the men's outhouse; football beyond the rows and rows of small tents people had pitched to sleep in. Noisy boys shouted as they played marbles by the meeting-tent entrance.

Giggly girls stood by the water pump where they gathered for drinks and hoped the boys would notice them as they passed.

Small children, and some not so small, swam on hot afternoons in the brownish waters of the old Ribstone.

The ladies took turns working in the dining tent. They peeled the vegetables and potatoes that farmers had donated. I've heard it said (and I don't doubt it for a minute) that they roasted a whole cow for Sunday dinner.

There were meetings, too—church meetings, three times a day, with no 20-minute sermons. Two hours was average. I never heard a complaint.

There were meetings, too—church meetings, three times a day, with no 20-minute sermons. Two hours was average. I never heard a complaint.

At some meetings missionaries told about their work. Some had come from Africa, others from India or China. They showed pictures of black people who lived in mud huts and talked in strange languages, or Chinese who dressed funny—little, short people, people who called, "Come and tell us about Jesus ere we die in our sins." More than once I decreed I'd go when I grew up.

There were meetings for children, meetings where Bible stories came to life, where puppets talked, where dummies and ventriloquists told stories and jokes.

Then came the serious services. A thousand people sang the old hymns of the faith.

When I shut my eyes, I could see the saints in heaven, standing around the throne of God. The throne sat under the Tree of Life on the banks of the River Jordan, and they sang the beautiful words of *Amazing Grace.*

Then came the preaching. The evangelist was an old black fellow from state-side. He came regularly.

His white teeth flashed against the darkness of his skin as he smiled. He stepped into the pulpit, bowed his white curly head, and began to pray. I'll bet God heard him, for you could hear him with human ears way down by the creek. When he lifted his eyes, he opened his Bible and began. He read and preached and then preached and read.

"Folks," he'd say, "there's a rumor rumbling

through the church. A dangerous rumor. A wicked rumor. A rumor that says there isn't any hell. Let me tell you the Bible says, 'There is a hell!' Why, Jesus Christ talked more about hell than he did about heaven.

"If there isn't any hell, then Jesus was a liar. He died in vain. Liars don't die to prove their lies. If there's no hell, there's no heaven either.

"Let me warn you, don't end up in hell before you find out that the rumors were lies from the devil."

He would step to the head of the platform and drop his voice an octave. "Folks, it's time to get right with God. If you choose Jesus, God and heaven, step out of your seat and come down to the altar to pray."

The aisles filled almost immediately. They were as crowded as busy city sidewalks during the Christmas rush.

Hard-faced men and ladies dabbing at their eyes with clean lace hankies all moved down the aisle together, all sorry for their sins and asking God to forgive them and vowing, with His help, to live a Christian life.

All week it was the same—Christians asking God to help them live a holier life—saints-that-ain't confessing their hypocrisy—sinners kneeling on the sod and crying, "God be merciful to me, a sinner!"

Yes sir, I even saw old Chuck Gee walk down those aisles and cry out to God.

As our team headed home from camp meeting, I couldn't wait for next year. Better yet, I couldn't wait to get to heaven and hear the saints all sing *Amazing Grace*. But then, like old Mac would say, "We've just experienced a little bit of heaven." ❖

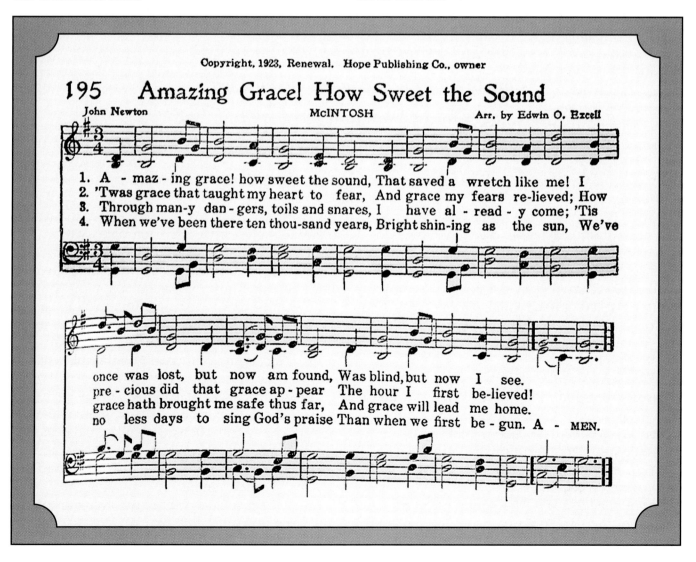

Ice-Cream Social

By Helen Colwell Oakley

*P*reparations were underway with a great flurry of excitement over the ice-cream social that would be held Sunday afternoon on the church lawn.

The ladies of the church joined forces by ringing up all the members on the crank phones to spread the word and to ask for volunteers to furnish freezers of homemade ice cream and other goodies. Those who made the freezers of ice cream almost always had a dairy to supply creamy milk for the ice cream. Those with a dairy usually had a flock of laying hens to provide the fresh eggs required for the delicious custard recipes. Some of the old-timers preferred the tried and true recipes handed down through the years from generation to generation while others made ice cream from junket tablets. "Junket tablets are too newfangled," Mom said; so the ice cream made at our house was made up from a cooked custard with eggs and cream and pure vanilla. Dad sold bottled milk in town, so we had all the milk and cream we could use, fresh from the farm.

The ice cream made at our house was made up from a cooked custard with eggs and cream and pure vanilla. We had all the milk and cream we could use, fresh from the farm.

The ladies of the church always made the desserts for which they were famous around the little village. One brought a delectable three-layer chocolate cake topped with crushed nuts; another furnished gingersnaps that disappeared like magic. There were tables full of fancy cupcakes, brownies, and a variety of homemade fudge. The young girls and ladies of the parish always wore gorgeous tea aprons of organdy, lace and ribbons as they waited on tables, serving ample portions to both young and old. All were dressed in their Sunday best: men in neatly pressed suits, white shirts, ties and, occasionally, white shoes. The ladies were resplendent in frilly gowns, silk hose and high heels, with the small girls and boys scrubbed shiny clean and spotless in their Sunday-school outfits.

The day of our ice-cream social was hot and humid. I well remember how delightfully cooling the ice cream was, and how the frosty glasses of lemonade were refreshingly satisfying. Everything cost 5 cents, with folks sampling most every treat. If a child ran out of money, the good-hearted folks most always could find a nickel or two to spare, or spot a cookie that was broken or a dish of ice cream that was going to melt if it wasn't eaten right away.

The men dipped the ice cream out of freezers packed in salt. Sometimes the ice cream stayed firm, but other times it was quite apt to melt. This seemed to upset some of the folks in charge of the festivities. The crowd didn't seem to mind when the ice cream melted down; some would drink it like wonderful creamy milkshakes and still enjoy it thoroughly.

One fellow who was a jolly sort always dipped out the ice cream. "Black, pink, white or yaller?" he would ask as we walked close to the ice-cream booth. The "black" was chocolate, "pink," strawberry, "white," light vanilla, and the "yaller," French vanilla.

Ice-cream socials were a treasured part of the old-fashioned times that we enjoyed wholeheartedly. ❖

The Box Social

By Clyde J. Devaux

T had started Sunday school at the Methodist church, a small frame building 1½ miles from our home. The congregation was mostly working people who worked for 10 cents an hour, 10 hours a day. They had to hold services nightly to collect enough money to pay expenses.

Due to the members' small wages, the congregation needed other means of income. One was the old-fashioned box social and another was the ice-cream social. For 5 cents they served a fair-sized dish of ice cream, and for 10 cents, a super size. It came in several flavors, and chocolate was the children's favorite. The ladies baked cakes and a generous slice was included with each order. Tickets were sold in advance, and my father, the local medical doctor, was called on by most of the children who were selling tickets. He generally ended up with 20 or more 10-cent tickets.

My brother and I were given an equal number to use and share with friends. It was then that we realized that we both had a broad circle of friends. We both enjoyed the opportunity to share with many underprivileged children, but that is another story.

The box social was the first I had attended. My father gave me the large sum of 25 cents to bid on a box. Single girls packed a lunch for two in a shoebox, then decorated the parcel like a gift. The most elegantly decorated boxes were chosen to be auctioned first and always brought the highest bids. Young men wishing to show off to the young ladies would go all out in their bids for the first several boxes.

I did not understand that when one bought a box, he was expected to share it with the lady who had made it.

I recall that the first one went for $1.50. That was equal to a day-and-a-half's pay, 15 hours. I was discouraged when I saw what the first several boxes sold for. But as the bidding continued, the prices kept getting lower until one box sold for 35 cents. Then the next went for 25 cents, and from then on, the boxes stayed at that price. It was then that I outbid a boy who had bid 15 cents.

By then, all the older men had bought their boxes. Only youngsters like me were left to bid. This, of course, was discouraging to the young ladies whose boxes were sold to small boys. They had all wanted to meet a "young man" (and this was a good way to do it), but not an 8-year-old.

I did not understand that when one bought a box, he was expected to share it with the lady who had made it. I found a chair and opened the box and found it well filled. I selected a cold boiled-ham sandwich and was about halfway through it when an older man told me where to find my hostess. She laughed at me for starting to eat by myself—and she was telling everybody near us all about it. This embarrassed me so much that I rose without a word and walked away.

I was soon located by the man who had told me that I was to share with the young lady. "I noticed that you didn't finish your lunch. Didn't you like it?" he asked.

I hung my head, speechless.

"Come now, what's the trouble?"

"She made fun of me because I didn't know I was supposed to let her have part of the lunch," I sobbed.

He patted my head. "Wait here," he said.

He soon returned with the young lady, who was carrying the box. She said she was sorry and hadn't meant to embarrass me. "Come on back and have some cake and a banana."

"I will if you sit somewhere else to eat," I answered.

When she asked me if I would rather eat alone, I answered, "Yes, but you can take your share out first."

"That's very considerate of you, but I'm not hungry," she said. "Why don't you find a friend who didn't buy a box and share it with him?"

That was no problem. Most of the kids I knew were from large families and never had even a few pennies, let along dimes or quarters. I looked about and saw several such boys. I not only chose one, but two. Then I let them divide the contents. That made me much happier than I would have been had I shared it with only one.

In our home we were not limited on the amount of food we ate. But in the poorer families, children were served one helping by their father, and they always left the table slightly hungry. They were always happy to share candy or apples at school with my brother and me. My father was very generous and gave us each a nickel each day for candy or gum, besides the apples or bananas that we carried for recess.

When the young lady and the gentleman saw what I had done, they both came to me and told me that I was a very considerate little boy to give up my share to other boys who had no money to make a bid. "I want you to know that I am glad you bought my box," the young lady said. "You have taught me a wonderful lesson in sharing. I am sorry that I embarrassed you, but glad about the way it turned out." Then she gave me a big hug and a kiss on the cheek.

The gentleman, who was a businessman, said, "This gives me an idea." The crowd was just finishing lunch. He called for attention.

"Brothers and sisters, we have a very fine example of charity given by a little boy." He then related the whole story about me. Nobody laughed this time.

"Now," he continued, "there are several boxes that have not been sold. I will pass the hat and we can buy the rest of the boxes with the collection. Then we will deliver the lunches to the boys who were unable to bid for lack of money."

When the collection was finished, he announced that instead of the lady sharing her lunch, he would let two of the boys share each of the several boxes that were left. The hungry boys were delighted to have such a treat. There were enough to supply all those present. The older members watched the boys devour the goodies.

The following Sunday, the minister talked in his sermon about how a little boy's embarrassment had taught such a lesson in sharing. I sat there blushing when he mentioned my name. I was happy, however, that I was responsible for a lesson I had unintentionally taught the older members—especially the young lady whose lunch I had bought. ❖

The Plum Silk Dress

By Blanche Floyd

"Isn't it pretty? You'll like the color," Mama assured me.

And I did. My new Sunday dress was the smooth, bright color of plum jam, just perfect with my dark brown hair and eyes. As usual, I tried to pretend that the big brown freckles were really not there.

I was 7 years old, one of eight children in a Methodist preacher's family. Getting a new dress was really an occasion in those days of the Great Depression. Proudly, I hung my dress in the closet along with my sister's clothes and my own skimpy wardrobe. I lovingly smoothed the shiny pleats and folds.

Sunday morning finally came and we were off to church, brushed and polished and dressed in our best. It was a cool, fall day, but I needed no coat. My new dress would keep me warm.

After church, we were invited to the Warrens' house to eat a huge Sunday dinner and visit awhile. They had lots of children and we loved visiting them. The younger children were allowed to sit on the porch after we ate and play quiet guessing games. We knew not to play rowdy games on Sunday, or to mess up our church clothes.

At the sound of cloth ripping, my first thought was of my new dress. My beautiful plum silk dress had caught a snag on the fence.

Tiring of quiet games, we moved away from the house to walk down to the creek. We stayed away from the joggling board set under the great oak trees. As much as we all loved to bounce on the board, we knew that we should not have that much fun on the Sabbath Day.

A low fence edged the yard to keep small children near the house and the cattle near the creek. The boys took the fence in one leap, but the girls walked sedately to the gate. Not me. Once the girls had turned their backs, the old tomboy in me took over and I went sailing over the fence after the boys—almost!

At the sound of cloth ripping, my first thought was of my new dress. My beautiful plum silk dress had caught a snag on the fence. There was a long tear down the side. I stumbled over to a rotting log, even forgetting the red bugs I was sure to attract, and sank down to inspect the damage. The tear was longer and worse than I had thought. What could I do?

When the parents called, we rushed back to the house and then to the car for our trip home. I pulled off my dress as soon as we got home and hung it carefully so the tear wouldn't show. My sister might tell if she saw it.

After our supper of milk, cake and fruit, we all got ready to walk over to the church again. I knew I would be expected to wear my new dress, so I put it on, lapping the tear over and pinning it. It was warmer than ever, but I put on my coat and buttoned it up. Then I brushed my hair, ignored my freckles, and went out with the brothers and sisters.

During the service, the church got warmer and I began to sweat. Mama motioned to me to take off my coat. I shook my head, but decided to unbutton the top button. As I settled down, the pin stuck in my leg and I bounced straight up. Mama looked my way and I eased down again.

So there I sat, sweating to death in my buttoned-up coat and bleeding to death from a pin scratch, with my lovely dress ruined. Daddy was saying from the pulpit, "Lift up your hearts! Be happy in God's beautiful world!" My misery increased.

School, play and chores took up my time during the next week, so I almost forgot about the dress. When I did remember it, I would screw up my eyes tight and whisper, "Please, God, don't let Mama find out I tore my new dress!"

Sunday dawned bright and fair and warm. What to wear? I looked at my old Sunday dress, inches too short. Could I bear to wear my coat again all day over my torn dress?

Reluctantly, I took down my plum silk dress and slipped it on. I reached for the rip, expecting to feel the pin again. But where was it? Gingerly I felt and looked for the long, ugly tear. It was gone. Had the whole thing been a nightmare? Was it a miracle?

I looked down at the skirt. The pleats swung

evenly in place and the dress was freshly pressed. From the door I heard Mama say, "Are you ready to go?" She was smiling at me.

And then I knew. Mama had fixed my beautiful dress so the tear didn't show. I flew to the door and wrapped my arms around her waist. "Thank you, Mama," I whispered.

She dropped a kiss on the top of my head and down the hall we went, gathering brothers and sisters along the way.

"I don't think I need my coat today," I sang, until the others made me hush. ❖

Homecoming

By Sarah Newsom

id-August was usually hot, dusty and dry. The crops were "laid by," as my father said. While the crops ripened, the farmers had several weeks of semi-rest before the harvesting began. We had a respite from sunrise-to-sunset work and time also for a spiritual revival. The second Sunday in August was "Homecoming" at the small country church I attended as a child. This was followed by a week of revival during which we attended church twice daily. Some of my fondest childhood memories revolve around those "Homecoming" days.

How eagerly we looked forward to that week of revival! Frankly, we were a bit more interested in the social aspects of the week than the spiritual ones. (In truth, the social life of the adults of the community pretty much revolved around church activities as well.) After a long summer of semi-isolation, this week gave us an opportunity to see our friends daily. Growing up in the country, as I did, meant not seeing friends on a regular basis once school was out for the summer. Homecoming week gave us a grand opportunity to catch up on summer gossip and to make our plans for the upcoming school year.

Homecoming Sunday was the big event. On this day, friends and relatives from afar returned to their childhood church. We'd see cousins and kin we scarcely knew, and we were "oohed" over, much to our embarrassment.

During the tiny summer break in the endless chores of farming came Revival Week, started off with Homecoming.

This was also the day that we had "all-day singing and dinner on the ground." Anyone who grew up in the South knows what a heavenly feast was spread on Homecoming Sunday. The women outdid themselves preparing their special dishes. Each had a specialty, and we'd wait impatiently for one of Aunt Velma's fried apple pies or some of Mrs. Smith's chicken and dumplings. There were heaping bowls of field peas, butter beans, corn, okra, squash and green beans. There were platters of firm, red tomatoes picked that very morning and jars of crispy, crunchy pickles. There were fluffy mounds of creamed potatoes and hot, homemade yeast rolls and brown, crusty corn bread. The baskets of fried chicken were there, of course, as were the smoked hams and sausages. There were watermelons in tubs of ice and gallons of hand-cranked ice cream and pitchers of iced tea and lemonade. The long tables set up under the trees groaned as much as the diners, who always overindulged and still regretted that they could not find room for just one more piece of lemon icebox pie. The food was the number-one priority to us children.

Once we had had our fill, we turned our attention to people watching. With awe and disbelief, we marveled at the "city folks" who had returned to their rural roots in their shiny new cars and fancy clothes. We children could scarcely conceive of the wealth that they must have had to travel in such style and dress so fine. Country folks did not wear coats and ties or nylon hose, hats and gloves to church in mid-August. Our cars and pickup trucks were old and covered with dust.

It was obvious that all the visiting ladies had been to the beauty parlor the day before. Just as obvious was the fact that all the "city" men wished that they could take off their coats and ties and roll up their shirtsleeves like the country folks did (country churches were not air-conditioned then), but they dared not. The doctor or lawyer or businessman from Memphis or Jackson or Birmingham had to show the old-timers that he had "done good" in life and he had to dress the part. That seemed to be what the old-timers wanted to see and the "city folks" never let them down.

The visitors stayed only for the Homecoming Sunday and the church was filled to capacity. Unlike the local farmers', their city jobs were not "laid by," so by midafternoon the city folks began their journeys home in their shiny new cars and coats and ties (rapidly removed before they reached the main highway, I'm sure).

Revival week was attended by the faithful few locals and the visiting preacher. There was always a visiting preacher who had to be fed. The women of the church took turns inviting him to dinner, which was the midday meal. When it was our turn to feed him, we had a slightly scaled-down version of the Sunday feast. He would stay and visit until time for the night service and we children had to be on our best behavior.

Since we attended church both day and night, we young people used the week as an opportunity to visit. We'd go home with each other after the morning service, visit all afternoon, and return for

Harvesttime Back Home

By Kathryn Thorne Bowsher

Harvesttime back home!
Sweet mem'ries those words recall
Of the warm and hearty welcome
At the old town meeting hall,
When good folk, from far and near,
Gathered on Thanksgiving Day
For fellowship and good cheer,
Meeting together to eat and pray.

The hall's old plank floor
With golden harvest was heaped,
Basking in bright autumn splendor.
Choicest crop that men had reaped
Was displayed for all to see,
When folks would congregate
To praise God for rich bounty,
Thank our Father for food we ate.

Long tables of pine
Held promise of sumptuous fare,
When we gladly sat down to dine,
Giving thanks to God in prayer—

Roast goose, turkey and dressing,
Cranberries, biscuits, sweet corn,
Mincemeat pie! Oh, what blessing,
Feasting together Thanksgiving morn!

In the afternoon,
From God's Word, the preacher read
How God sent His beloved Son,
Jesus Christ, Who died and bled.
Rafters rang with joyous song
As we sang praise to God above,
For saving men from sin and wrong
By His immeasurable grace and love.

Blessing fell on all
Within that hallowed place,
The revered old meeting hall.
Gladness beamed on ev'ry face.
Fed on manna from above,
From our Father's storehouse rare,
Hearts rejoiced in His great love,
Worshiping God in song and prayer.

the night service. Sometime we were even allowed to spend the night with our friends. What a treat that was! We'd spread pallets on the floor and laugh and talk far into the night.

It has been years now since I've attended a revival at a country church, but the memories linger. I can no longer sing *Amazing Grace* or *What a Friend We Have in Jesus* without looking at the hymnal as I once could. I no longer have to be on my best behavior because the preacher's coming to dinner. That, of course, is my loss. But come the second Sunday in August, I hope I'll be one of the "city folks" who travels the country roads to that small country church of my youth. Somehow I'll find room for that one last piece of lemon icebox pie. ❖

Dinner on the Grounds

By Eunice J. Pitchford

"Dinner on the grounds" has been a Southern church ritual for generations.

It relates not only to church traditions, but equally to the traditional family reunion.

I have heard church-going stories from my mother who was born just before the turn of the century. Her family descended from the Scots and Irish who brought their Presbyterian faith to this country.

Because of distances between Presbyterian churches in Guilford County in central North Carolina, they were among a group who pulled away to form a new church midway between the two already established. With members forced to travel either by foot or horse-drawn vehicles, travel time and distance were problems.

In early days, the rural churches were lighted only by oil lamps, and circumstances didn't lend themselves to evening worship services. On special occasions there were both morning and afternoon services. Families brought along food for Sunday dinner. ("Dinner" then means "lunch" today.) Eventually some churches built picnic tables and some constructed shelters over the tables.

One elderly friend recalls her family bringing their very best tablecloths—linen or cotton damask bleached sparkling white—and spreading them on the ground for their meal. She said they got really progressive when some of the men of the congregation figured a way to suspend tables by wires from sturdy tree limbs!

In the late 1920s and early '30s, my father took his parents in his Model-T Ford (and later in his 1928 Oldsmobile sedan) on a two-hour trip to attend an annual memorial service at a church where their immediate kin were buried. Fresh flowers were taken to adorn the graves that day. The services in the church were held as usual in the morning and the memorial service was held in the afternoon. We were present for dinner on the ground between the two services.

I remember long tables assembled end-to-end and loaded down with many platters of fried chicken, potato salad, pickles, sliced tomatoes, sandwiches and pies and cakes galore. My sister never forgot the vivid pink of one cousin's cake; heavy use of food coloring must have been the lady's trademark.

In the days before interstates and rest areas, when our family was on a summer vacation trip, we looked for churchyards on rural roads for our lunch stops. They offered a safe place away from traffic, and on a weekday the picnic table would not be in use.

Today I live in the North Carolina mountains during the summer. I regularly read notices in the Hendersonville newspaper of homecoming services at churches and "dinner on the grounds" is always part of the notice, a carryover from yesteryear.

Another notice I frequently read concerns family reunions. The location may be given as a family member's home, a church, or a civic building, but it will then give the family name followed by the time and "dinner on the grounds."

Convenience may have been the beginning of tradition, but the pleasures keep it alive. ❖

Church Wasn't Boring Then

By Merlin Wilkins

W henever I am introduced to a group of people as "Rev. Wilkins," someone is invariably startled enough to blurt out, "You are a minister? You certainly don't look like one." "Thank you," I reply in mock seriousness. "You are very kind." I admit that I am pleased with the mystery of that remark, for few people would understand why a person belonging to the profession would at the same time divorce himself from the typical man of the cloth. Well, it's just that when I was very young and growing up in a minister's home, I witnessed a constant parade of oddball sizes, shapes and personalities who billed themselves as evangelists. It was these characters who, at my father's invitation, roomed with us for two weeks and conducted the fall revival, the winter revival, the spring revival, or the summer tent meetings in the town park. No one could say that church was boring.

My father selected their names from the advertising sections of the various religious magazines to which he subscribed; thus, all of us got to meet the messenger of God for the first time. It got so that we all tried to predict what the next one would be like. No image was beyond our imagination, for we had already seen what we believed to be the freaks of the religious zoo. Dr. Potts, for example, who inspected the ceiling all during his sermon, never had time in the afternoon for pastoral calls because he had to play golf to exercise his "middle third." Wee Willie Grant averaged one fit of epilepsy per week and tried to make us believe he was in a trance. Who could forget C. Wentworth Black, who could double for Frank Burns, of television's M*A*S*H? C. Wentworth was a chaplain in the Army Reserve, and carried a .38-caliber automatic in his suitcase. He had a supply of wax bullets that he fired to fend off marauding flies. He also made pastoral calls in his uniform.

Mr. Moon liked to tease me, but I did not realize that it was not the prerogative of a little kid to reciprocate.

Less weird but equally interesting were people like Swede Carlsen, who ate so many snacks each day that my mother was a nervous wreck trying to keep him filled up. For years, I thought all Swedes ate six meals a day instead of the usual three. Later came Methodist Sam, a Serbian immigrant whose egotistical mien would make Muhammed Ali

look like a shrinking violet. His sermons ran the gamut from how smart he was to how poor and dirty he used to be, to how he could annihilate a man with only one punch. He is one of my all-time favorites; he convinced me that he was a real man who brooked no nonsense from anyone. Not many religious types have impressed me so since.

The favorite of most of the kids was a 5-foot pixie named Mr. Moon. Each night he drew a crowd of kids to church to watch his magic tricks; tricks he used to keep our attention while he made some theological point. He would show us an empty cup, for example, and then pour a glass of water into it. While he told us about the limitless nature of God's blessings, he would fill an entire pitcher with the contents of the cup. I think we really believed that God enlarged the water supply.

Mr. Moon liked to tease me, but I did not realize that it was not the prerogative of a little kid to reciprocate. One night while he was telling us that God was able to supply all of our needs, even our food, he dramatically produced a string of wieners from inside his shirtfront. I stared a moment at his ample belly and then yelled from the front row, "So that's what you have in there! You better not take out any more or your pants will fall down!"

The laughter had not yet subsided when my mother whisked me off the pew and carried me home to bed. Neither she nor my father was laughing, so I couldn't either.

Nothing lasts forever, though, and the parade was no exception. It was killed, as you might expect, by one of its own, a flamboyant type named Bob Wilson. His nickname was Holy Bob and his main claim to fame was some vague connection he had had with Billy Sunday, the same Billy Sunday who was the model for Sinclair Lewis' evangelical hypocrite, Elmer Gantry. I suspect now that Billy Sunday was also the model for Holy Bob Wilson, for like Sunday, he drew enormous crowds to watch him dramatize his illustrations. They laughed when he made fun of sin and sinners and cried when he related, in a quavering voice, the hopeless plight of a fine woman and her small children, struggling pitifully to survive in spite of a drunken husband and father. He always had, as the saying goes, his audience in the palm of his hand, simply spellbound.

It was the last night of his meeting, though, that did it. By tradition, a "love offering" was taken on the last night for the evangelist, and most people brought a little extra money along for just that purpose. My father made the customary announcements, called the ushers and received the offering. From then on, nothing was customary.

Holy Bob left the platform and inspected the offering and did not care a bit for what he saw. "Now listen, folks," he said, "I've labored among you for two weeks now, pouring out my very

By tradition, a "love offering" was taken on the last night for the evangelist, and most people brought a little extra money along for just that purpose.

heart and soul in order to lead you to heaven. Is this the paltry thanks I get?" He pointed and thundered, "You and you and you should be ashamed! It won't do! Ushers! Come back here; we must do this again!"

Startled but obedient, the ushers passed the plates once more and once more Holy Bob pawed through the bills and loose change. What he saw dismayed him.

"Folks," he began, as if he wanted to cry, "I've a good notion not to preach tonight." Again he pointed and his voice now thundered, "You have not robbed me; you have robbed GOD!" He waited for that to take effect, and then he lowered his voice and continued, "We will pass the plates once more now. I want you to be honest with God. I want you to open your hearts and your pocketbooks. God will not bless the niggardly. Try to keep what you have and God will take it from you."

He suddenly ceased his threats when he saw that my father was livid with rage. Bob quickly announced that the local pastor, my father, would receive Bob's tithe, a tenth of the offering, but the damage was done, and Bob didn't dare check the offering the third time. He went back to the business of saving souls as if nothing had ever happened.

It had, though. My father never answered another ad. An era had passed, and as far as I am concerned, a certain amount of color passed from the religious scene, as well. Now when I hear somebody complain that church is dull, I want to say, "Hey, I can remember when it wasn't. Let me tell you about an old Serb who came to this country when he was 10. He'd never had enough to eat, never slept in a bed, and when they gave him his first bath, he was bleeding in over a hundred places. No one messed with him either; he could lay a man out with one punch. ... " No, they'd never believe it. They are right; the religious scene is dull nowadays. ❖

Protracted Meetings

By Florine F. Hudson

In the little churches of yesterday, worship was simple and sincere. The definition of protracted is "prolonged; extending over a long period of time." Protracted meetings were an annual event in the churches of our area during my childhood and early adult years. At "laying-by time," meaning the end of working crops until harvest began, farmers could take time to attend protracted meetings at the local church.

Shiloh Baptist Church near Aiken, S.C., was my home church. Neighboring churches scheduled their meetings so there was no conflict. We visited other churches on Sundays during their protracted meetings and their members visited us. There was no conflict; we were all neighbors and friends.

The first Sunday in August was the beginning of our church's six days of meetings, Sunday through Friday. Sunday was the big day. Just about everyone came, if they were close enough to get there in a buggy or wagon.

Sometimes we had a visiting preacher, but not always. Since we had services only once a month during the year, we were glad to hear our own preacher for a series of services.

We had Sunday school and preaching on our regular meeting days during the year so this Sunday was no different. The service went from 10 a.m. to noon and reconvened at 1:30 p.m. During the week, services started about 11 a.m.

When we arrived at church, there was a parting of the ways. The men might linger on the outside to talk to a neighbor. When they went in, the men took the left side and the women turned to the right. A few might get their directions confused and sit on the wrong side, especially if it was a young man whose intentions were to sit with a certain fair lady.

Mothers of small children often brought a canning jar of water and some tea cakes to quiet the children in case the preacher was long-winded. Some of those morning sermons could get lengthy.

Afterward, the men helped get the baskets and boxes of food to the long wooden table under the shade trees near a cool spring of water. My first memories of these meetings were before the "ice age" so we had to depend on this spring for cool water. No iced tea in those days! We had bountiful meals. Cooks were known for their special dishes. Except for cakes and pies, the food was cooked just before going to church. The chicken had to be dressed and cooked the same day. Remember, this was August. We had the most dedicated gnats in the country. They came to every service in droves and joined us at the table for dinner, too.

During the intermission between morning and afternoon services, some of the teenagers collected money for the preacher.

After dinner, the crowd assembled in the church for the afternoon sermon.

If there were conversions during the year, they were held over until the first Sunday in September. At this time, all who joined the church were baptized in the spring after dinner. The water was just plain cold. If all baptismals now were as cold as that pool, I expect there would be more baptized-by-sprinkling Methodists.

This way of worship was not a hardship but a way of life leading to a more meaningful relationship with God and our fellow man. ❖

What Are All Those Round Baskets For?

By Patti Ann Griffin

It was the summer of 1945. My brother and I were exploring around Grandma's farm. From somewhere in the distance we heard singing, drums, tambourines, all kinds of wondrous sounds. My brother, who was 10 years old, five years older than I was, started walking toward the music. I yelled, "Tommy, wait for me!"

My brother and I spent the summers of 1943, '44 and '45 (during World War II) at Grandma's farm in Terre Haute, Ind. The farm was a whole different world for two little city kids from Milwaukee, where we lived in a nice neighborhood in a little bungalow on a city-size lot. We were used to all the modern conveniences—indoor plumbing, electricity, hot water, gas stove, etc.

Mother sent us to Grandma's because she needed to continue to work full time in the summer; our dad was in the Army. She wanted us to be well cared for and Grandma loved us, so …

We couldn't see what was being put into the baskets, but we could hear jingling. As the baskets were moving, the people were singing.

It was a rude awakening upon arriving at Grandma's to find only a pump outside the kitchen door, and an outhouse (which scared me to death). And, although the farmhouse was wired for electricity, the local co-op had not reached Grandma's yet.

But children are adaptable and it didn't take us long to get used to the "medieval" conditions. We didn't realize that other people lived like this. We thought only our grandma and Aunt Bessie (my mother's sister) did.

The next morning after breakfast (Grandma fried potatoes, eggs and bacon like no one else), we were assigned chores. After our chores were done, we were free to do anything we wanted, as long as we had permission. The rules being laid out for us, we soon settled in.

On that day when we heard all those magical sounds, we had asked permission to take a walk. It was one of those lazy summer days made for children. Grandma consented, but said we could only go as far as her voice would carry, whatever that meant.

"Tommy, wait for me," I whined again.

"Well, hurry up or I'll ditch you," he answered. I scurried, half-running to catch up.

"Where are we going?" I asked.

"To the carnival. Can't you hear the music?"

"We'd better not," I said. "It's going to get dark soon." It was just about twilight—that magic time of day when anything can happen. "We won't hear Grandma if she calls," I said.

"You're such a baby. Don't be such a scaredy cat. It'll be fun. Come on, hurry up!" Tommy urged.

It would be worth a switching to get a peek of where that music is coming from, I thought to myself.

Off in the distance, we could barely make out an orange structure of some sort. We were walking hand in hand. The last strands of daylight were wisping away. As we looked up, the "thing" materialized into a gigantic orange tent. Two tall torches guarded the front entrance. The whole scene looked like something out of *Arabian Nights.*

But what was going on inside? What an adventure! It was not a carnival, that was for sure. As we drew near, we could hear singing, yelling and low moaning, all at the same time. Now, even closer, the tent took on a life all its own. The entrance became a gaping hole, the tent took on an ominous look, more than scary, and yet …

Tommy and I looked at each other, wide-eyed with wonder. Almost simultaneously we ducked down on all fours, crawled under the tent wall and peeked inside. We couldn't see much— mostly feet tapping, feet and legs running up and down the aisles.

Next thing we knew, we were sitting on a bale of hay at the end of the back row nearest the tent wall. It was deafening—people shouting, music playing, the choir in front dressed in white uniforms and singing. People were running up and down the aisle; some fell down and rolled on the ground, and others were jumping up and down.

Some were falling backward as a man dressed in a long white robe touched their foreheads. Some were caught before they hit the ground; others weren't. My brother and I were mesmerized— what a show!

Suddenly, the man dressed in white stretched out his arms. The crowd settled down. He said, "Do you believe?"

The crowd answered together, "We believe, we believe!"

The man in white then said, "Show how you believe with your love offerings!"

Suddenly, as if on command, 12 men (one at the end of each row) passed a round wicker basket down each row. We couldn't see what was being put into the baskets, but we could hear jingling. As the baskets were moving, the people were singing.

Finally, the basket went past us—almost. We saw more coins and dollar bills then we had ever seen before. Tommy reached in and grabbed a handful. We slipped off the hay, ducked under the tent walls, went past the huge torches and started running for all we were worth. We were scared almost out of our wits. Suppose they came after us? We had no idea where we were or where we were running. Now, we were terrified.

The light of the torches was gone now. It was pitch black. I started to sob. "Hush, hush," my brother cooed. "It's OK! Look, we're rich! We have $2.75." Even in the dark, the coins glimmered. I stopped crying and pointed to a pinpoint of light.

"Tommy, let's go over that way." We still thought we were being chased, and we started running again. We headed for the light and miraculously landed in my grandma and Aunt

Bessie's open arms. I was never so glad to be held, to be safe.

"Where have you children been? We've been so worried. It's dark. You didn't come when we called," Grandma said, with great concern in her voice.

I started to tell Grandma what happened to us. As I described the scenario, she started to smile and Aunt Bessie laughed out loud. I described the people rolling around, jumping up and down. I told them about all that money.

That's when I knew we were in trouble. Up til then, Tommy and I were doing all right, but when I told Grandma we had the small fortune of $2.75, her expression changed from amusement to pity. She said, "Come now, children, we have to take this money back to who it really belongs to." We looked at her in astonishment. We had risked our lives for that money. No way were we going back there again; that's what we were running from!

On the way back to the tent, Grandma explained what we had stumbled into and what really had been going on. She understood our curiosity and terror. She understood how we had been enticed by the music and hymn singing coming from the revival meeting. That's what the tent was all about.

These revivals were held for people who had no recognized religious affiliation. No matter how strange it seemed to us, the people were expressing their love for God.

She went on to explain that the running, jumping and speaking in tongues, which we had interpreted as moaning, were expressions of their belief in God. They believed in God and loved Him as much as we did, only in a different way. Her explanation proved to be very precious to me all my life. It was a lesson in religious freedom.

These revivals were held for people who had no recognized religious affiliation. No matter how strange it seemed to us, the people were expressing their love for God.

Now the hard part came. "Grandma, do we have to give it back?" we asked.

"It belongs to the Lord," she answered. We approached the tent. It didn't look scary now. Everyone was gathered around, talking about what a nice service it had been. We walked way behind Grandma and Aunt Bessie. Grandma approached the minister. She explained we were visiting her and had no idea what a revival meeting was.

"Tommy, Patti, come here," she called. We went very slowly to Grandma's side. "Give the money to the minister." The minister stretched out his hand. Tommy dropped the coins into his palm. "We didn't know," Tommy whispered. The minister gave us an understanding smile.

We returned to Grandma's house. It was late. We were tucked into our feather beds with loving hands. The last thing I remember saying that night was, "Grandma, will we get a switching?"

She answered, "You've paid dearly for your misadventure. Now go to sleep. God bless and sweet dreams."

Needless to say, we never again went out of reach of Grandma's voice or stayed out after dark. Well, almost never. ❖

Singing Conventions

By Clara Haggard Comstock

One of our favorite social gatherings was the "singing convention." Several communities would plan "singings" for a certain Sunday each month from May 'til September. Now, this was actually a competition, and each community practiced every night for weeks before to prepare. There were quartets, duets, family groups and other specialties besides the main attraction, the church choir. Each tried to outdo the others with new songs, unusual arrangements and the perfection born of long hours of practice.

Everyone liked to be in on it, but some didn't want to bother going to practice. It was pretty disgusting to practice and have it down pat and then have it ruined because one or two who hadn't practiced held a note right through a rest stop.

As we started off to the "singing," the wagons would travel together. Young people would sit on blankets thrown over the hay, and grown-ups would sit in cane-bottom chairs. If you were really lucky and weren't "too little," you were allowed to sit in the back with the gate down, dangling your feet out. In your best slippers and a ruffled white dress and swinging your feet—well, it was the height of your glory!

We'd all shout back and forth, and sing, too. When we got there, the place would already be alive with people, everyone calling, "Hello! How are you?" Papa would unhook the team, take them to the back of the wagon and give them a block of hay. We'd all go into the little church or school (my new shoes squeaking), and I'd sit with Mama so I could help with the little kids.

Papa always led the singing, and in the morning hours, everyone joined in and sang together. You've heard of "raising the roof"? I think this might be where the expression started, because when they all sang, you'd swear that roof might fly right off. Those folks would really sit back and sing—and they were good singers.

At noon, they had "dinner on the ground," as families and friends set dinner together. They'd spread a red-checked tablecloth on the ground and someone would brew a pot of coffee on a campfire. Several would walk about to sample all the food, and there was time for a good visit.

After the food was put away, the contest began. Each group would sing three songs and judges chose the best. No actual prizes were awarded—the winners were just "named" first, second and third best—but they couldn't have worked harder if silver cups had been at stake.

There was always respectful admiration from the others as each group sang. Once, three of Papa's brothers came in unexpectedly and with Papa, they made up a quartet. With Uncle Neely on guitar, it just about turned into a "hoe-down" dance with much clappin' and stompin'. Of course, there never was a Haggard that couldn't sing. They used to say that when a Haggard baby was born, it didn't cry; it sang, "Do, re, mi."

The trip home was fun, too, as we'd raid the dinner basket (Mama had always brought enough food for that, too). Then the little kids would go to sleep. The old spring wagon would squeak and bump over the rocky roads. We'd drop off Henry and Margie Howell, and watch Edna and Liza get out and run home.

There was nothing quite as exciting or satisfying as our "singing conventions." ❖

Remember the Old Church Songs?

By Irma Dovey

In my youth, 40 years ago, the music used in church was different from what we hear today. It was informal, it had swing, and it spoke to the heart.

Do you remember some of the old songs? In our church we sang out of hymnals, and yet we distinguished between "hymns" and "Sunday-school songs."

A hymn is defined in the dictionary as "a song of praise to God," or "a metrical composition adapted for singing in a religious service," and "a song of praise or joy." By these standards, the songs we sang at home were all hymns.

Some had solemnity and a majestic ring even when sung by only 20 worshipers in our small-town church. Such songs as *Holy, Holy, Holy, All Hail the Power of Jesus' Name* and *Come, Thou Fount of Every Blessing* were truly moving.

I suppose today we would call the other songs "folksy." In Sunday school, and sometimes in church, we sang *What a Friend We Have in Jesus, Brighten the Corner Where You Are, Jesus Loves Me* and *Tell Me the Old, Old Story.* You can get quite a jazz movement out of Brighten the Corner if you play it with a good swing, and perhaps this is why the children always loved it.

Shall We Gather at the River? is a song often associated with funerals, but to me it is part of my early childhood. My mother always sang this song through tears, apparently thinking of friends and family members who had gone before.

In our church, these two were sung often, lovingly and lingeringly: *Blessed Be the Tie That Binds* and *Break Thou the Bread of Life.* Some groups reserve these for communion service, but we did not.

As a teenager, I played the piano for congregational singing, and was happy with any minister who respected my level of ability by giving me a slip of paper each Sunday with four easy songs listed on it. We often sang *Blessed Assurance, Faith of Our Fathers, In the Garden* and *Jesus, Lover of My Soul.*

> *I played the piano for congregational singing, and was happy with any minister who respected my level of ability by giving me a slip of paper each Sunday with four easy songs listed on it.*

My mother sang and whistled hymns as she worked around the house. These included *Ring Dem Bells* and *Whispering Hope*, songs she had sung many years before in a traveling quartet that visited neighboring communities.

Perhaps my family background and my experience in a church in a town of 200 people tell why I am nostalgic over the old melodies. I go to a large city church now, with organ music, a robed choir and a full-time music director. Some of the choir songs are from cantatas or are musical showpieces. I respect and admire the musicians for their skill, but often I hunger for the hymns and Sunday-school songs we sang at the old home church. ❖

Pumping Up the Pulpit

By Bernadine F. Wells

*P*raise the Lord and Pass the Ammunition was a popular song during World War II, and it could have been my mother's theme song when she pumped the small, single-keyboard organ in our little country church.

If you had known my mother and watched her during Sunday-morning services, you would agree that she praised the Lord in a most warlike manner. When the sparrows scattered from the steeple, we didn't know if they were frightened or if the rattling of the rafters shook them from their roosting places. As Mom rambled toward the organ, clutching her cloth handbag, we dared not breathe until she straddled the small, round stool. There wasn't a stool made to fit her posterior.

She arrived early, as it took a long time to get the stops pulled to create just the right sound. Then she made sure her feet were placed on the pedals in the proper position and her knees spread apart to give sufficient pressure to the knee levers.

Mom was ready to begin the minute the Rev. Jackson walked to the podium, adjusted his glasses, and gave her his quick nod. Her feet started pumping, her knees pushed in and out, and her stubby fingers raced across the keys. The louder the congregation sang, the faster Mom pumped, pushed and rocked on her little round stool. The perspiration rolled from her brow, and when she gave a certain wiggle, we knew it had begun to trickle down her spine.

Sunday morning was the highlight of our week. It was social as well as spiritual—all because of Mom's pumping and pushing on that little organ. On those rare occasions when she slowed to a softer melody, we heard Mr. Jones' collie harmonizing from across the street. I was in my teens before I realized it was Rover and not Miss Lena Wilson as she strained for those high notes.

Weddings were always festive with relatives and friends coming from throughout the county. When Mom pumped and pushed, *Here Comes the Bride* was never delivered with more sentiment. She pushed, pumped and wiggled on her little stool until the bride and groom were well on their way to a long and happy married life. At times, Mom got so carried away, the bridal party stood for several minutes in front of the altar until the Rev. Jackson loudly cleared his throat and signaled that it was time to stop.

Then there were the funerals. If it were possible for anyone to enjoy funerals, it would have been my mother. She had a special black dress and a small black hat, which she perched atop her gray hair. One of her favorite hymns was *Nearer My God to Thee*. She pumped and pushed in a doleful manner that caused the bereaved family to mourn and weep all the more.

Now that Mom has departed this life, I'm sure she has managed to sneak in a small organ somewhere up there. Often at night, when I hear the rumble of thunder, I know she's shoved the harps to one side and is pumping while the heavenly choirs sing alleluia. ❖

Wonderful Summertime Sundays

By Lorraine B. Shaw

Raised by a loving grandmother in a tiny, mid-Illinois town during the 1920s and '30s, I have many warm memories of those truly Good Old Days! As I thread my way home through the heavy, late-Sunday traffic, I enjoy daydreaming about the placid Sundays spent on my favorite uncle's farm. There, most of the traffic plodded down tree-shaded dusty roads that muffled the slight creak of buggy axles dried by heat and dust. Everyone knew everyone else, usually by the team hitched to the buggy.

As they approached the farmhouses, the teams would slow; the folks in the yard would leave the shade to greet the buggy which might be coming to call or merely going by on another visit down the road. Sometimes on hot days folks would drive the buggy on in and drop reins at the big oval horse tank to let the team lip up a refreshing drink while the occupants would alight to enjoy a glass of fresh-squeezed lemonade and exchange crop talk.

Sunday was an unhurried, happy, lazy, well-fed day—and I loved it!

Summer Sundays began about the same time as other days of the week, with Grandma waking me: "Wash and set the table! Biscuits is bakin'!" I'd had my Saturday bath in the big washtub on the back porch the night before, but it was still mandatory to "wash" in one of the enameled basins set on a long table beside the cistern pump in one corner of the kitchen.

Grandma usually had chores to take care of in the chicken yard or vegetable garden, or even picked a bouquet for the sitting-room table.

I'd dress in everyday clothes first, wash up quickly and dry my hands and face on the huck roller towel, then set the usual three places at the big round kitchen table where Grandma, my uncle and I ate our meals.

In summer, Grandma used a kerosene stove instead of the big, black, wood-burning range, but food still tasted just as good because it had Grandma's special touch. Her sourdough biscuits raised high and light. The crock of apple butter was spicy and cold from the cellar, as was the round of butter. The sugar-cured bacon from Uncle's smokehouse would be fried to an unmatched crispness in the big iron spider, followed into the skillet by golden-eyed eggs Grandma brought in from the henhouse out in the backyard.

Coffee was already bubbling aromatically in the gray-speckled "granite" pot on one burner, and bacon cooked slowly over a lower flame on the middle burner. At first Grandma had disliked the kerosene contraption, but once she got used to adjusting the heat, she welcomed the relief it gave from an overly hot kitchen. Only when it was canning time did she fire up the big range for the day, starting it off with kerosene-soaked corncobs, then adding wood and a few lumps of hard coal. Luckily, those days were later in the summer or in early fall, and her day would begin at dawn when it was coolest.

By the time breakfast was on our plates, the summer heat was already bearing down. Though the windows were open for air, the dark green blinds were down so the rest of the house had a dusky, jungle look except for the bright squares of doorways to the front and back porches. As we ate, the big teakettle heated dishwashing water. Grandma and I would make short work of the dishes—my job was drying them with big hemmed squares of bleached flour or sugar sacks, then hanging the sopping-wet dish towels and dishrag on the ever-present "line" strung across the back porch. I'd have time to play with my cat before getting dressed for Sunday school. Grandma usually had chores to take care of in the chicken yard or vegetable garden, or even picked a bouquet for the sitting-room table.

When my country cousin's touring car rounded the corner and pulled up under the big maple trees in front of the house, I'd be ready to join them for the usual trip across town to their church. My girl cousin and I would look each other over, comment on our dresses or new hair bow, socks or hankies. I had short hair, flaming red to match my freckles. Her hair was "long enough to sit on" and worn unbraided only on Sundays, falling in a heavy cascade of crinkles from a neat center part punctuated by crisp ribbon bows. I envied that beautiful head of hair and bows; she envied me the lighter weight of bobbed hair.

At the church, she and I

entered our basement Sunday-school room, her brother going to another room nearby, the parents solemnly entering the sanctuary at the top of the broad cement stairs.

During Sunday school, with windows open above and below, we could hear the dramatic vibrations of the sermon, the wafting hymns, sometimes even the tread of the deacons walking the aisles with their red velvet baskets on long wooden poles, collecting the offering. We had our own offering, of course—coins tied into one corner of a clean Sunday hanky. I often had another knotted corner of coins donated by my uncle to spend on penny candy at the drugstore as my girl cousin and I walked the few blocks home. As we walked, her parents and brother would drive to the icehouse, where a huge oblong chunk of ice would be wrapped in a green tarp and tied to the running board of the car.

We'd usually arrive simultaneously at Grandma's house, where I'd quickly change from Sunday-best to clean, everyday clothes for the trip to the farm. Uncle rarely went along since Sunday was his day to lounge around the stable and harness shop in our backyard, joined by his old cronies from around town. He would have been downtown, however, for the Sunday paper, leaving the funnies for me to take along for afternoon reading and re-reading with the cousins. Sometimes, if he'd earned a little extra that week fixing binder canvas or harness for the surrounding farmers, there'd be a pack of Beeman's Pepsin Gum with the funnies.

Hurrying to prevent any additional melting of the ice, Grandma and I would get into the car, wave goodbye to Uncle and my cat, and after the required number of deliberate shiftings of the black-knobbed stick under the car's steering wheel, we'd be off! A few blocks from Grandma's we'd stop as Ginny's dad looked both ways, down, up and down again the two-lane "hard road." Then, with a bump and a great shifting of gears and a smell of gasoline, we'd be up, on and rolling down the road with summer breezes blowing our hair and whipping

PERSIS CLAYTON WEIRS

our voices as they billowed the canvas top of the leather-seated touring car.

It seemed a long journey, though it was less than 5 miles to Uncle Fred's, with our top speed somewhere in the range of 15 miles an hour, I imagine! Eventually, however, his big, square, gray house would loom on the hill ahead, and we'd slow down at the orchard, making ready for the sharp turn between high-cut banks onto the lane leading to the back gate.

Our arrival was always as if we'd just returned from a world tour. Aunt Addie would kiss me and Ginny, and try to kiss Cousin Ray, who was too big a boy by then to be mushed over, even by his own grandma. Uncle Fred was in clean bib overalls and blue denim shirt, and was clean-shaven except for his moustache (which I referred to as "shredded wheat"). He would take charge of the cake of ice, lifting it easily from the car into a big tub under the shade trees, then covering tub and all with old comforters and horse blankets to delay melting. We could smell chicken frying and bread baking, along with a bouquet of other delectable odors coming from the kitchen and big dining room.

Once we had been suitably greeted, Aunt Addie and Ginny's mother (who was my first cousin) would bustle into the kitchen to bring out the wooden ice-cream freezer and the tall can filled with creamy custard. The older boys by then would have a gunnysack and mallet ready to crack up the ice, and another sack of coarse salt to layer into the freezer. Uncle Fred, as usual, supervised the procedure, and they took turns cranking until it became so hard to crank that it was obviously time to "lift the dasher" and see if the ice cream was ready. Licking the dasher was a shared treat with us three youngsters, once Uncle Fred had spooned off a taste for approval. Then the can was packed solidly in more ice and salt, covered with more blankets and left to ripen while we trooped into the big, airy dining room.

What dinners those were! Big platters of

fried chicken and biscuits; a crusty loaf of bread on the cutting board with a murderous knife for slicing. Dish after dish of pickles, relishes and jam or jelly. Big bowls of buttered green beans and wilted lettuce with bacon bits in tangy vinegar dressing. Platters of steaming "roastin' ears," pickled beets and coleslaw. Golden balls of fresh butter as big as half grapefruits. Pitchers of iced tea and lemonade, and one of cold buttermilk for Uncle Fred. Creamy chicken gravy for the heaped bowls of fluffy mashed potatoes. Ah, that was living! And there was always pie, cake and cookies. The ice cream was a midafternoon treat to spoon out of bowls as we relaxed in the shade.

After a dinner like that, relaxing was the order of the day, except for the women, who cleared the table, scraped chicken bones and

Grandma and Uncle would chat about the news from the farm and whatever city gossip he might have gleaned during the day.

corncobs into the swill bucket for the hogs, and washed the piles of dishes, glasses, pots and pans. Only then did they join the men on the lawn or sink into rockers on the shady side of the porch. Leftover food was covered with a cheesecloth fly-cover and left on the table for supper, or placed in the honest-to-gosh icebox if perishable.

Ginny and I would read the funnies, play paper dolls with the special box kept on the lower shelf of the library table or, if there happened to be a new family of kittens in the haymow, walk slowly to the barn and climb the steep ladder into the dusty, fragrant loft, listening for the tiny mews to lead us to the kittens.

Midafternoons were hot in Illinois, but it was always comparatively cool under the canopy of 100-year-old maples, elms and walnut trees in the farmyard. Grandma would fan herself gently with one of the cardboard fans handed out in those days by local funeral parlors. She was so tiny—less than 5 feet tall—that a special low-seated rocker was always moved out of the "front room" for her. While the men dozed and womanly conversation lapsed, the only sounds were the swish-swish of the fan and the slight creak of the rocker.

An old blanket on the grass was Ginny's and my domain, with the funnies spread in front of us, or one of the ladylike projects kept on hand for our visits: quilt blocks to stitch, or balls of string and the wooden-peg pot-holder loom. We kept all three households amply supplied with pot holders. And by the time we were 12, each of us had completed enough blocks for a quilt of our own, to be "tied off" at the big frames during the winter when adult quilts were done.

By about 4 o'clock, the ice-cream can had been emptied and the last crumbs of leftover cake consumed, along with whatever else we might have wanted from the table. Then it was time to start for home so that Ginny's parents would be home at milking time. Tired and full of good food, we'd slump in the backseat, Ginny's hair again braided and looped up with an everyday bow, our once-fresh percale dresses crumpled and sweaty from the heat. Grandma would hold the special plate of goodies reserved for my city uncle on her lap, her starchy sunbonnet tied under her chin again. Her apron was folded neatly on her lap under the wrapped plate of cold chicken, pickles, pie, cake and other tidbits—a feast Uncle would share with me when he joined us for light supper that evening.

After such a bountiful day, Grandma would make a pot of tea, set out cold biscuits, a wedge of sharp cheddar cheese, and cut a few slices from the stick of summer sausage that hung inside a cheesecloth bag down cellar. She and Uncle would chat about the news from the farm and whatever city gossip he might have gleaned during the day. By then fireflies were skimming through the dusk and my cat was seated beside the back door, his tail curled around his feet, awaiting his share of the food.

After a short swinging session in the wooden two-seater on the front porch, inhaling the combined fragrance of blooming flowers and Uncle's mosquito smudge pot, it was time for bed. Almost stumbling in my weary, near-sleep state, I'd get into a nightie and slide between crisp, line-dried muslin sheets, crunching a little as I settled into the straw-filled "tick" that replaced winter's warmer feather bed. Before the last light was out, my cat would scamper indoors and settle onto the foot of the bed, as happy and tired as I was after another long summer Sunday.

The Good Old Days aren't really gone—not as long as they're tucked away in memory to take out and relive again when the pressures of our hurried, worried world bear down! ❖

Decoration Day

By Ruth Ann Leatherman

Things were different on Memorial Day when I was a child. The first obvious difference was the name of the day itself. We didn't call it "Memorial Day"; it was always "Decoration Day," and we did just that—we decorated. Graves of soldiers and loved ones were treated equally with love and tenderness.

The day in my section of Kentucky was observed on Sunday in church instead of Monday.

My memories of childhood Decoration Days are of things that happened not so long ago, but yet a lifetime away. Time has faded the sad memories but left the happy memories vivid and bright.

Those memories are topped by the times spent at all-day preachings and dinners on the grounds.

Here is what Decoration Day spent in Flatwoods, Ky., was like.

Preparations began two weeks in advance. Graves were cleared of the rubbish dumped on them by the previous winter. Women filled cupboards with pies and cakes in anticipation of the event.

We traveled to the church at Aunt Maggie's house in a pickup truck, the only accepted mode of transportation in those days. We crossed the creek when the road did and thought nothing of it. After all, creeks have a right to run, too.

Everybody who was going to the service in the little church on top of the hill stopped first at Aunt Maggie's house. The reason was simple. You couldn't get up the steep hill with anything but foot power.

We traveled to the church at Aunt Maggie's house in a pickup truck, the only accepted mode of transportation in those days.

This type of all-day meeting was as much social as it was religious. We saw all the cousins we hadn't seen for months, kissed all the aunts and learned all the new babies' names.

Playing with the cousins was the highlight of the day for my sister and me. As most of the cousins were girls, a boy cousin was a prize and demanded respect and a place of honor among his admiring young female relatives.

We had one special cousin we called "Old Joe Crow." Let me assure you, he was not named after any Kentucky-type beverage. Our innocent minds would not have taken us that far in those days. We called him Old Joe Crow because he entertained us by perching on a chair and crowing like a rooster. Oh, how we admired that boy! I don't remember why we called him "old."

Around 10 a.m., all the faithful began the journey up the steep hill to the church house for the service. Little groups of "brothers" and "sisters" congregated outside the door until time for singing.

The church house was a miracle in itself. It stood on a steep bank supported by flat rocks as the only foundation. It is amazing that the little white building didn't tumble down the hill when the good sisters began rejoicing during the worship.

Our church was a lively affair. People believed church should be something you enjoyed. Isn't it a shame we know better now?

After we sang from the Sweet Songster for about an hour, the first preacher got up to speak. He would stamp his feet and point his finger while branding on our minds the punishment for sin.

The "Amen corner" would lend their support; the sisters would clap; the babies would cry and then things started to get noisy.

Someone would start a song. Another would give out the song, which means a leader would throw out the words to the congregation and they would repeat after him. Before the service was over, everyone would be standing, shaking hands and hugging one another like they really lived by the love preached in the sermon.

My sister and I enjoyed the service, but two sermons were enough for 8- and 10-year-olds. We knew the precise moment to ask if it was okay to go outside to play. When the service had moved far enough along that the mothers were thinking more about worship than making the kids sit still—that was the time to make the getaway.

We bolted out to an ancient walnut tree and waited for the cousins to make their escape. When four or five had gathered, the fun began.

First, off came the shoes. Oh, the pleasure of toes released from the prison of Sunday shoes to wiggle in the dust of time in the old churchyard! We played in the woods close to the church so when the last song was sung, we could slip back inside and avoid a disapproving glance from the fathers.

After church, the Decoration Day observance began in earnest. A solemn procession made its way along the path to the graveyard. (Another difference: It was "graveyard," not "cemetery.")

After prayers and remembrance of the dead, dinner was served on the grounds. Chicken and dumplings, pickled beans and corn bread were served up by loving hands. Those old-fashioned meals were brought to a satisfying end with apple stack cake and blackberry cobbler. Hot dogs on the grill were still a decade or two in the future for the observance of this summertime holiday.

With dinner over, we were free to wander among the ancient tombstones and wooden crosses. The older people would remember Great-Aunt Bessie and Old Uncle Abe and decorate their graves with flowers picked from the hills they had walked during their sojourn on earth.

Around 5 p.m., we made our way down the steep hill to Aunt Maggie's house. The evening was spent in more singing and sometimes staying overnight with the cousins.

Yes, it was different in those days. No parades march across my memories, and the only public speeches were given by Brother Joe Sparks in the little church.

I returned for a visit to the church about years ago. It was still standing and in use. I wondered at the flat rocks that had held the church so steady for so many years.

I realized the same Rock that steadies that old-fashioned regular Baptist church, attended by English descendants, "soft-shell," is the same Rock that steadies the American Lutheran church of German descendants I attend today. That Rock is Jesus Christ.

Things are different. Times have changed, but the feelings of people who observe Memorial Day or Decoration Day are the same in the flatland of Ohio I now call home as in the hills of Kentucky where my memories live. ❖

A Lesson for Lori

By Winifred L. Thompson

On a Sunday in January 1916, my friends Nora and Jake, who were three and four years older than I, came to the front door and asked if I could go sledding with them. Mother said, "Of course not, it's Sunday!" So they left. She was quite strict about keeping Sunday a real holy day.

We were having chicken and biscuits and gravy for dinner. This was special; we didn't have chicken very often and when we did, it was always on Sunday. My mouth was watering just, thinking about dinner. This didn't keep me from getting into my outdoor clothes very quietly and sneaking out to the porch for my sled while the rest of the family was in the kitchen preparing the feast.

I quickly joined Nora and Jake, and we had two grand runs down the hill, over the tracks and down into the meadow with our sleds.

I don't know whether the sled was mad at me because it wanted to rest on Sunday or not, but the next time I went down the hill, the fool thing just wouldn't steer right and ran wham! into the bench where people sat to wait for the streetcar.

My head jerked forward and the soft underpart of my chin hit the sharp corner of the bench. I was cut but good, and a little dazed.

My friends helped me up the path to my house and onto the porch. They knocked, and when Mom came to the door, Nora said, "She got hurt sledding." With that, they both took off as though they were going to be chased.

Mom quickly got a towel. I was bleeding all over everything. She got things under control and called our doctor, who said he would be up on the next streetcar. He was there in an hour.

Dad was so nervous that he got ready and took the streetcar down to the armory in the city where he worked. His job would be called "maintenance engineer" nowadays; back then he was just a plain "janitor," but a very good one.

When the doctor came, my sister put on her outdoor clothes and went out to sit in our outhouse. Mom had fixed it up very nice— papered the walls, put carpeting on the floor and on and around the seat. We had both a crescent moon and a star on the door!

Mom said, "You are going to have to have stitches; I will call Mrs. Burns, the practical nurse, to come and hold your hands."

Begging her not to (Mrs. Burns was so fat and I had always been a little afraid of her), I promised to be real good.

Well, the doctor fixed my face and I didn't holler, even though he sewed me up without giving me anything. When he was through, he said, "You were a very brave little girl. How old are you?"

I raised one hand and showed five fingers and two fingers on my other hand. My face was pretty well bandaged and it hurt to talk.

He said, "Why, that's how many stitches I had to take. Aren't you glad you're not 10?"

I just nodded. After Mom gave him a cup of tea and paid him, he left on the next streetcar.

She called my sister to come in, and called up my Dad to come home. Then she looked me straight in the eye and said, "Guess you won't go sledding on Sunday again."

I couldn't say much, but two tears rolled down my cheeks. As Mom bent down to gently wipe them away, she kissed me and said, "I'll save you a nice piece of white chicken and some biscuits and gravy for tomorrow. You should feel better then."

So ended a Sunday that gave the streetcar company some extra business and taught me a hard-earned lesson in obedience. ❖

> *My head jerked forward and the soft underpart of my chin hit the sharp corner of the bench.*

Saved From Our Sins

By Marie Parker

Is there anyone out there old enough to remember the old-fashioned tent revival? Tent revivals were miniature Billy Graham sessions held in the summer months underneath the trees. It was the Depression and everyone needed all the uplifting they could get.

The flies and mosquitoes were the first to arrive, so as not to miss anything or anybody. Those bites, plus a liberal sprinkling of chiggers, gave us kids the appearance of a chicken-pox ward. Add to that our gaily patched clothing and you have a gathering of very average little souls, as innocent as babies and as ignorant as goats.

Nobody told us we needed shoes, socks, clothes and haircuts, not to mention an extra biscuit now and then. We came into the world with nothing and it looked like we were going out the same way.

Whichever neighbor didn't have their water cut off gave the rest of us some to water down our soup. We would fight the dog, tooth and claw, for a bone from the butcher shop. One might say we were poor.

All the neighborhood gang (ages 7–9) perched piously on the front benches. Not through choice, however. Our suspicious parents were sitting right behind us. The local undertaker supplied us with paper fans.

"Look at all them flowers," one scroungy little fellow said. "That's what you get when you die!" All of us were familiar with the bug-ridden wildflowers, but we had never been exposed to roses and high-class flowers.

After the novelty of the paper fans wore off, we would play tic-tac-toe with our bare feet in the dirt. Usually, one or more of us would have a kerosene-soaked strip of cloth wrapped around a toe. We never went to a doctor. To us, the doctor was omnipotent, ranking about second from God with his white coat and education.

Our parents knew how to get our attention with the old familiar "melon thump." You snap the fingers sharply against the culprit's head, and if he jumped, you knew he was alive and would henceforth be attentive. Sometimes we would all get restless at the same time and the thumping would make regular choir notes, depending upon the thickness of your hair.

The fiery young preacher was a hellfire-and-brimstone type, but we all just loved him. He looked so kindly at us kids and pretended not to see our little diversions.

The fiery young preacher was a hellfire-and-brimstone type, but we all just loved him. He looked so kindly at us kids and pretended not to see our little diversions. And, believe me, we could think of more diversions than General George Patton could. We were listening at the same time. Don't ask me how; how do teenagers study with Van Halen raising the air around them 50 decibels?

The next day we would all get in a huddle and recount our sins. We were really impressed by this preacher and we sure didn't want to go to hell. Our confessions were pretty grim. We decided that we were just about as sorry as you can get. We had cheated, swiped marbles, and cut that grouchy old Mrs. Clay's clothesline. We had lied to our parents, each other, and anybody else who had us on the carpet.

Some of these confessions had repercussions. "You mean you stole my aggie marble, you little creep?" Then two or more kids would choose up and fight like two dogs in the dust.

One of our group was a little beast named Frances. She didn't play with us much, as her mother figured that would be like pitting the Flying Nun against Hell's Angels.

Anyhow, we didn't like the way she flaunted her white shoes and socks (in the summertime, yet). My brother once lost a mate to a pair of socks and we put a thick coat of mud on the other foot and made the day nicely.

Frances observed the two dusty gladiators and said loftily, "I'm going to pray for you." Whereas the two culprits blinked, arose from the dust, and chased Frances Pureheart all the way home.

The next night we'd all be back on our perches at the tent revival again. Sure enough, by then our tender little hearts felt a terrible burden of guilt and we all marched rank and file (some more rank than others) down to Brother Aylee to tell him how awful we were and to just kill us if he thought we needed it.

Then a very sweet expression crossed his face and he provided a handkerchief to wipe the tears from our sinful, dusty little faces. This made us feel so pure that sometimes we were good all the way home.

One night, a very drunken old man leaned against a tree off in the background, several yards away. I understood bootleg whiskey in a "dry" county didn't go down smoothly—it more likely embalmed you or gave you the blind staggers. This was one sin none of our gang knew anything about. Anyhow, the drunk came night after night, crying out loudly.

"Come into our meeting," our good, kind preacher called out to him.

"Oh, I'm not fit, I'm not fit, I'm no good," he would reply. Evidently he wasn't, as he showed up the next night, same tree, same shape, same refrain.

This was during the Depression and preachers traveled fast and furious, far and wide, to try to help the depressed people and probably to prepare them for the afterlife in case they starved to death.

Well, we survived it. I hope that wherever Brother Aylee is, he knows his motley little bunch of marble stealers and liars never forgot him. And we even forgave Frances. ❖

Day of Wonder

By Red Ricker

After 74 years, I still wonder why Grandma O'Neil took me along on her trip to the city. It was a short trip, only 8 miles, but it must have been quite an adventure for one who seldom left the homestead where we all—parents, grandparents and children—lived under one roof.

We didn't go by horse and buggy, and we didn't go by automobile. Grandpa had bought a new 1918 Chevrolet, but on his first expedition, he'd hit a hitching post in front of the nearby church. Mortified, he never touched the vehicle again, and Grandma never learned to drive. So we began our journey on foot.

On that bright, sunny day, we walked a mile or so to the foot of our hill. There we picked up the trolley car line, which we could take 7 miles east to the town of Hummelstown, or 7 miles west to the city of Harrisburg. We rode in style to the city, where we walked a few blocks to the big white tent where a traveling evangelist was holding services.

Grandma was about 90 percent deaf. She wore a hearing aid with a big battery that hung on a cord around her neck, and when I spoke to her she could hear me only if she turned up the power all the way.

When the preacher invited those with infirmities to come forward, she needed no urging. She went up and was touched—and she heard.

On the way home, Grandma was as lively and animated as a schoolgirl. I know she could hear because we talked with the hearing aid tucked in her purse. Exactly what was said I can't recall, for this was long ago when I was only 5, but our conversation was light and easy.

The restoration of Grandma's hearing was perhaps temporary. My grandfather, a highly educated man and a skeptic, scoffed at Grandma. He didn't believe in miracles and he was embarrassed, I think, to be so close to one.

A few days after her cure, Grandma went back to wearing her hearing aid. Had she lost her ability to hear, or was she pretending so as to calm her husband? I wonder. I'll never know, but I know that I believe in miracles because I was with Grandma on the day one took place. ❖

A Wedding at Camp-Meeting Time

By Alvin Peterson

The best of years and the worst of years was 1914 out on the Summit, S.D., prairie. It was summer and very warm. The wind blew day and night, never seeming to stop. It sent ripples and waves across the tall prairie grass, transforming it into a great sea. My brother and I, ages 11 and 14, were experiencing one of those grand old tent meetings. There was much singing, but no instruments to sing with. There was great preaching, the kind that made one tingle all the way down to his toes, the kind that really brought conviction.

The tent in which we met was a big one, almost like a huge circus tent, with planks for seats. They rolled up the sides of the tent on those very hot evenings to allow the breeze to blow through. Those were great meetings.

As the evangelist wound down a bit, the mind would wander and one could look out across the tall, waving prairie grass. Suddenly wonderful illusions would appear; the waving grass would suddenly become water, and the tent was the ark of safety. The daydreams often seemed more exciting than the preaching, but all of it mixed together became the greatest of recipes for some very precious memories.

One very special night, after the evening service, there was a wedding right in that tent! A neighbor and his blushing bride came right down the aisle. It was quite an exciting moment. The tent was filled; horses and buggies completely surrounded it that night. There was no wedding music, but suddenly everybody turned and the benches creaked as the happy couple walked down the walkway to the front.

To a couple of farm boys, that wedding seemed extra special, almost as good as the Founder's Day celebration over at Ortley. But then, almost as quickly as it had begun, it was all over. Everybody was leaving, congratulating the bride and groom and hitching horses to the wagons and buggies. It was during this confusing time of loading wagons and buggies that a neighbor boy came running with the exciting news that there was going to be a square dance to honor the bride and groom in the newlyweds' barn. The news spread like wildfire from one rig to another. There was going to be a good old hoedown!

The word spread to everybody—everybody, that is, but the preachers. They were purposely left a bit in the dark, for they had made it quite clear during the week that dancing was the devil's pastime, something to be avoided at all costs.

My brother and I (and apparently a lot of other people) had not listened too closely to the preachers' words of wisdom. The temptation was too great; we had to go to that square dance.

It was quite a square dance. Up the steps we went, into the haymow. All around the walls of the barn and roof were benches and old straight-back chairs. People were visiting everywhere, talking about the weather, the crops, the wedding and a hundred and one other things.

A man was playing a fiddle, stomping his foot to keep time. Another man was calling the square dance. He yelled out at the top of his voice, "Twenty couples up for the dance!"

Just at that very moment, to the horror of a good many there at the dance, the preachers walked by the open haymow door. What a moment that was for some of the good folk at the dance!

After the dance was over, two very tired boys hurried home to tell the news of the exciting evening to our folks. But when we got home, we got the shock of our lives. The preachers had come to our house to spend the night!

That night we slept a troubled sleep. We awoke in the morning with a mixture of fear and horror in our hearts. At the breakfast table, we faced the preachers' piercing black eyes. It was quite a moment of self-examination, to say the least, a moment never to be forgotten.

The couple who were married that night went on to have quite a family. I think they had 15 children in all. It started with a square dance and ended with a roundup. They were a wonderful family, one my brother and I enjoyed very much out on the Summit prairies. ❖

Our New Shoes

By Marguerite Getz

*D*uring the mid-teens, I was just a kid, growing up along with my two sisters on a farm in southwestern Ohio. We went every Sunday to worship in a little country church in a village about a mile from our home.

One Sunday morning as we were leaving the services, we had no sooner unhitched our horse, climbed into the surrey and started homeward, when my father made a very emphatic statement.

"That preacher made a big mistake when he scheduled a midweek special revival service during corn-husking time. The weather has been bad, the days are getting shorter, and all us farmers are behind in getting the corn out of the fields before winter. We haven't time to go to any weeknight revival meeting and I'm not going."

They were of the very latest style— black patent leather at heel and toe, with high tops of white leather and a row of black buttons all the way up the sides.

Mom never said a word, but my sisters and I had a good idea what was going on in her mind. We knew Mom well enough to know that if there was a service going on at that church Wednesday night, she would be there.

And we also knew that if Mom went, her three daughters would be there with her. And we wouldn't fuss about it, as we always liked to dress up for church.

We never went there without putting on our Sunday-go-to-meeting clothes, and little girls did enjoy dressing up. To top it off, we each had new shoes for fall and winter. They were the very latest style—black patent leather at heel and toe, with high tops of white leather and row of black buttons all the way up the sides. We were so proud of those new shoes and happy that our mother had a new pair like them.

She had said no more to our father about church, but had arranged with our neighbor lady to walk there with her and her three daughters.

When Wednesday came, Mom, with our help, milked the cows, fed the chickens and had an early supper while our father was still working with our hired hand in the field. We left their meal in the warming oven of the old range, wrote them a note, and took off for church.

We were soon down our lane and joined by our neighbor friends as we started up the road to the village. A new layer of crushed stone had recently been put down on that road to keep it from washing away during the wet weather of winter and spring.

By summer it would be a good, hard-surfaced road, but we found it too rough to walk on, especially in our new shoes. So we took the narrow path by the side of the road.

We must have looked like a string of geese as the eight of us walked along single-file, being very careful to step over puddles left from a recent rain.

When we arrived at the village, we noticed that there was a lot of excitement at the corner grocery, and a crowd of people had gathered there. As we came nearer, we saw that a peddler was putting on quite a show to draw people closer before he opened his pack to sell his wares. He was playing an old guitar, singing funny songs and dancing about, and the kids were stamping and clapping along with him.

All the grown-up people were enjoying the fun. The peddler had previously visited the old saloon across the street and he was in fine shape to entertain his audience.

People were forgetting the time when, all at once, we heard two taps of the old church bell. The crowd suddenly dispersed, dashing out the door and down the street to the church.

We found a small crowd already assembled, and the preacher up front was wearing a very stern face. My sister hurried to the old pump organ and got ready for the opening hymn while others found their places in the choir loft or in their pews.

We had a late start, but when that preacher got started he was really wound up. We had a long, powerful, hellfire-and-brimstone sermon. In fact, it lasted so long that when we left and walked through the village, the grocery store was closed and those not at church had gone to bed.

The moon was shining as we left the town and started down the road. We had gone a short distance when someone said, "What's that dark thing down there in the middle of the road?"

Right then, two women and six girls got scared. Not taking time to investigate, we all took off in a dead run past that dark mound. We never thought of new shoes or going

single-file as we ran pell-mell, smack-dab right down the middle of that road! Stones flew and water splashed but we never slowed until we reached our neighbor's home.

We went in to catch our breath, rest awhile and assess the damage we had done to our clothes. When we got under the lights and looked at each other, we didn't know whether to laugh or cry. Our new shoes were so scuffed up and covered with muddy water that they looked like they had seen tough wear for many seasons.

Next day, we heard about that dark mound we had seen in the road. It seems that the poor peddler was so hurt after his crowd left that he went over to the saloon and had another drink or two before leaving town. As he went down the road, he passed out, and there he lay until he awakened next morning and went on his way to the next town.

We have laughed through these many years as we've thought about it and we've told this story to our children, grandchildren and great-grandchildren. We always say, "Oh, that was the night we were entertained at the grocery store, revived in church, and scared half to death on the way home!" And the sad part was, we ruined our new shoes to boot! ❖

Shall We Gather at the River?

By Danny C. Blevins

I remember they sang *Shall We Gather at the River?* and that they were there for one reason: It was the will of the Lord.

Old men were there with creased hats and graying hair. Elderly ladies came with tears in their eyes but smiles on their faces, and young couples walked hand in hand and watched as the children played by the water's edge. They had all gathered by a not-so-sacred river for the holiest of ceremonies, a baptism.

From among the crowd of spectators, three young boys came and stood by the water's edge. Their slightly worn overalls quivered with each shake of their nervous legs, and their eyes searched the crowd for family, friends and perhaps reassurance. For just as John the Baptist had baptized Jesus Christ in the river Jordan, so would these three young men be baptized.

Slowly the crowd settled down and from them emerged a minister and a deacon of the church. They walked down to the water where three boys stood with folded hands and bowed heads.

Deliberately, the two holy men of the church entered the water and by and by the minister raised his hands for silence.

"Brother William, will you please lead us in a hymn?" he trumpeted so all could hear.

"Do you believe that you have been saved by the Lord Jesus Christ?" Nervously, I nodded my head.

"Of course, Brother," replied Brother William. "Will everyone please turn your hymnals to 373?" And then, with voices of thunder, they sang *Shall We Gather at the River?*

As the singing died away, the minister stretched forth his hand to the first boy who had made a profession unto God. The boy slowly entered the river and all eyes watched as his arms shook from the cold water. Taking the boy by the hand, the minister leaned forward and whispered something into his trembling ear.

Nervously, the boy nodded. Placing one hand on the boy's shoulder and stretching forth the other as if trying to touch heaven itself, the minister proclaimed, "Having accepted the Lord Jesus Christ as your Savior, I now baptize you in the name of the Father, the Son and the Holy Spirit!"

With this, both the minister and the deacon took the boy by the arms and lowered his entire body into the water and then raised him out. Soaked from head to toe and sobbing uncontrollably, the boy sloshed to the riverbank and into the joyous arms of a thankful mother.

The next boy in line quietly slipped into the water with head lowered in mournful consent and humbleness. Again the minister whispered a question into the young man's ear and raised his hand toward heaven in divine proclamation, and he too was baptized.

As the young boy walked toward shore and toward me, thoughts raced through my feeble brain and butterflies fluttered and took flight in the pit of my stomach. Deep within, my faith began to waver. Looking at the minister's outstretched hand, I eased a reluctant foot into the water and made my way toward the two men who were waist-deep in the muddy current.

As the cold water crept into my shoes and numbed my feet, I placed myself in the hands of the awaiting men and the minister placed a reassuring hand on my shoulder.

Quietly he whispered to me, "Do you believe that you have been saved by the Lord Jesus Christ?" Nervously, I nodded my head.

At this he once again raised a hand to heaven and proclaimed in a thunderous voice, "Having given yourself to God, I now baptize you in the name of the Father, the Son and the Holy Spirit!"

I felt a gentle tug as I was lowered into the water and a surge as my feet rose toward the surface. For a split second, the water blocked out all creation, and it seemed as if I was about to look upon the face of God Himself. Then I was up.

Walking toward the bank, I took the minister's handkerchief and tried to wipe my eyes. Then I looked up and saw my mother standing with a towel neatly folded in her hands and tears streaming down her cheeks.

Falling into her arms, I hugged her. My own tears began to fall, and they came as if from a spring flowing from heaven itself.

For a few precious seconds on a beautiful Tennessee riverbank in mid-July, I felt closer to my mother than I ever had before or ever have since.

Today, stored neatly in a forgotten crevice of my existence is a memory of a river, and of a loving mother who wiped the river silt from my hair and dried my tearful eyes. The Good Old Days of yesterday were never better. ❖

A Country Baptism

By Elinore McCune

The shore-side congregation was singing as the minister grasped my hand and led me toward the slow-moving current until we stood waist deep in the slightly muddy waters of Grand River. "I baptize you in the name of the Father, and of the Son and of the Holy Spirit. Amen," he intoned. He supported my thin little shoulders and head with his left arm and dipped me backward so that the cool water closed over me and I seemed to be lying on the bottom. He had covered my face with a folded handkerchief and I had closed my eyes. Slowly he raised me to a standing position and we waded to the bank in the hot sunshine.

This is how my baptism came about: Our family, consisting of parents, three girls and a boy, lived in a crossroads town in northwest Missouri in the early days of this century. We always attended Sunday school. Our congregation was so small that we did not have a regular preacher but were "supplied" by one of several retired ministers who were sent by a church board in a larger town some 50 miles east on the Wabash Railroad. On a Sunday, one would ride up and hold a service, have dinner with a church member, then return on the late-afternoon train.

Shall we gather at the river,
Where bright angel feet have trod,
With its crystal tide forever,
Flowing by the throne of God?"

On this particular summer morning, a small, thin, somewhat defeated little man had arrived. The previous Sunday, my teacher had talked to our class about joining the church. The parents of six little girls had agreed. All had reached 12, the age of accountability, except me. My sister was 14, but I was only 11. However, it was concluded I was old enough to be committed.

Thus, when the congregation sang its invitational song, *Jesus Is Calling,* six little girls rose and filed solemnly down the aisle to the confessors' bench.

The minister was surprised and disconcerted. Mixed with his joy at saving souls must have been a mental question, How are we going to manage an immersion on such short notice—and what will I wear?

But our teacher had already made arrangements. A member had brought an old black suit; a farmer had promised a wagon bed filled with clean straw; several families had offered to drive carriages as few people had cars. Our teacher would take songbooks and we would assemble at 2:30 at the river nearly 3 miles away.

As soon as church services ended, we hurried home. Mother began to fry the chicken she had killed and cleaned on Saturday and salted down in a crock in the cellar. She warmed other food in the coal-oil-heated oven.

As planned, my sister and I each put on two petticoats, a white dress and long white stockings. Using big safety pins, Mother pinned our skirts between our legs so they would not balloon up onto the surface of the water.

As I put on my black patent-leather slippers, I wished momentarily I had a chunk of leftover breakfast biscuit to shine them with, as my seatmate at school claimed she did. But that would have been wasteful.

The white ribbon on my pigtail on one side had come loose. Mother rebraided my hair, retied the ribbon, then arranged the last few inches into a curl. With a damp brush, Mother would brush the hair around her forefinger, slip the curl off and caution me to be careful until it dried.

As she brushed my hair, Mother reminisced about her own baptism many years earlier. It had been in March, when cold temperatures had caused a thin skin of ice to form around the edges of the millpond where the ceremony took place. I knew that pond well. I stood on the footbridge above it on my way home from school on winter days and watched the big boys skating.

Recently the mill had caught fire and burned for many hours. Part of the earthen dam gave way, and the pond was now too shallow for religious ceremonies.

So, at the appointed time the serious little girls in white rode to the river in a wagon bed while other people rode in buggies or carriages. We drove over the bridge, then down on the west side to a shady strip of narrow rocky beach.

As everyone sang, the minister walked slowly into the water, testing the depth with a long narrow pole. After sticking it in the bed of the stream, he waded back to the bank and took each little girl in separately for the ceremony. My sister was first and I was last. As each girl was returned, her mother wrapped her in a quilt or a blanket.

The assembly sang, *Till We Meet Again,* and was dismissed with a prayer. People streamed back into town, the minister had time to change and meet the evening train, and six sanctified little girls were trundled home, having been assured their souls were saved for all eternity. ❖

That Old Cross

By J.B. Cearley

A young evangelist had a song for the world.
"On a hill far away … "
Almost halfway around the world from the Jerusalem hill of Golgotha, where Jesus was crucified, George Bennard wrote his immortal hymn, *The Old Rugged Cross.* Today a fitting memorial still stands in the tiny village of Pokagon, Mich. Visitors often turn off the scenic M-51 highway halfway between Niles and Dowagiac to view the crumbling monument in the abandoned old churchyard. The decaying structure has since been replaced by the Pokagon United Methodist Church, which stands across the street from the old sanctuary.

On Jan. 13, 1913, the Rev. L.O. Bostwick, pastor of the Pokagon Methodist Episcopal Church, penned a letter to the Rev. George Bennard of Albion, Mich. Pastor Bostwick had felt an urge to hold a series of revival meetings and invited Bennard to preach. Bennard accepted the invitation and arrived in Pokagon with a lyric he had been working on.

Shortly before being called to Pokagon, Bennard had undergone soul-searching contemplation of the importance of the cross in Christian life. He realized that the cross and Christ were one, entwined in a verse of scripture: "For God so loved the world, that He gave His only begotten Son, that whosoever believeth in Him should not perish, but have everlasting life" (John 3:16).

When his father died of coal-mining injuries, George quit school and began working in the mines to support his mother and four sisters.

Bennard had already titled his hymn *The Old Rugged Cross.* The evangelist then began working on the body of his song, but he was having difficulty with the words. As he prepared for the Pokagon meeting, Bennard picked out the melody on his guitar, constantly changing the wording. He would walk into the kitchen and sing the words with Mrs. Bostwick.

One afternoon, Bennard appeared in the kitchen and announced that the song was complete. He sang the finished product for the Bostwicks.

On a hill far away
stood an old rugged cross,
The emblem of suffering and shame;
And I love that old cross
where the dearest and best
For a world of lost sinners was slain.

Silence followed, and Mrs. Bostwick spoke softly: "That song will surely win the hearts of people everywhere."

That evening, Bennard sang the new hymn for the congregation and taught it to the choir. Florence Jones played the organ, accompanied by Arthur Dodd on the violin. Forty years later, *The Old Rugged Cross* topped the polls as the favorite hymn of the American people and remained there for several years. Mrs. Bostwick lived to see her prediction fulfilled.

George Bennard was born in 1873 to Scotch-Irish parents in Youngstown, Ohio. When his father died of coal-mining injuries, George quit school and began working in the mines to support his mother and four sisters. He was only 15. He later married and, as a born-again Christian, enlisted in the Salvation Army for eight years, playing the drum during services and learning to play the guitar.

Bennard was as enthusiastic with a small audience as he was in a large auditorium. He gave unselfishly of his time and energy, and he had a great love for people and his evangelistic message.

He resigned from the Salvation Army in 1907 and moved his family to Albion, N.Y., to become a traveling evangelist and minister of the Methodist Episcopal Church.

In 1918, Bennard became hard-pressed for money and sold the hymn to Homer A. Rodeheaver, who wrote hymns and traveled as a choir director for the popular evangelist, Billy Sunday. The Rodeheaver Company, founded by Billy Sunday, revealed that Bennard was paid more than $5,000 before he died; his widow continued to receive royalty payments every three months.

In 1953, Bennard was invited to attend the Rose Bowl Parade in Pasadena, Calif. He rode in a flower-covered float and played his masterpiece on a flower-decorated organ for the largest audience he would ever have.

When Bennard's health began to fail, he retired to Reed City, Mich.

In 1954, the Reed City Chamber of Commerce erected a 20-foot rough wooden cross near Bennard's retirement home as a tribute to the author. Soon afterward, Bennard was buried in Englewood, Calif.

George Bennard, who often said he hoped to be remembered as a Gospel minister rather than a composer, was added to the list of composers in the Gospel Music Hall of Fame in 1976. But to the thousands who have been moved by *The Old Rugged Cross,* this may have been his greatest sermon. ❖

Saints, Sinners & Samaritans

Chapter Four

Daddy had disdain for folks who were "Sunday Christians"—those who showed up for church routinely, but who failed to exercise godly virtue the rest of the week. He taught me from early in my life to be the same person seven days a week, 365 days a year, saying, "You ain't gonna fool God."

Many of the spiritual lessons I have learned in life I learned away from the confines of church and pulpit, and at the feet of saints, sinners and good Samaritans. You know who I mean—the everyday folks whose examples, both good and bad, mold our thoughts and actions.

As a toddler my spiritual guides were parents and grandparents. My universe expanded slowly into our extended family of aunts, uncles and cousins and finally into the big world of neighbors, townspeople and school chums. Some of the lessons I learned in that world were good; others I have spent a lifetime trying to unlearn.

Janice and I married when I was 21 and she barely 18 (fairly common in rural areas back in the Good Old Days). Saints, sinners and Samaritans pulled us through rough times and taught us how to rejoice in the good times.

In middle age I rediscovered the wisdom of my father—the wisdom that the arrogance of youth sometimes refuses to recognize. Late in his life Daddy showed me the Way more perfectly and purely than I surely could ever show my own son. Then he was gone.

Now that gray hair has invaded my own crown I find Daddy's wisdom is still out there, again in the words and deeds of saints, sinners and Samaritans—and I hope I always learn from them.

I now have arthritis in a bad left knee, so kneeling doesn't come easily—a condition with which I'm sure many of my readers of *Good Old Days* magazine can identify. In 1994 I published a poem in *Good Old Days* by a saint of a

woman, Ava Lois Halstead, "You Don't Have to Kneel to Pray." From her simple, pure words I was reminded again of the value of father and mother, grandfather and grandmother—be they saint, sinner or Samaritan.

—Ken Tate

You Don't Have to Kneel to Pray

By Ava Lois Halstead

Today a question was asked of me—
"Grandma, how do you kneel to pray?"
This is what my grandson (who's only three)
asked of me today!

"Your knees won't bend like they used to,
so you can't kneel on the floor.
There's so many things you used to do
that you can't do anymore.

"Now, I can bring you ice for your tea
and go get the mail for you,
But Grandma, do you want me
to kneel down and pray for you, too?"

I told him, "I really don't have to kneel
or even bend my knee,
for it doesn't matter when I make an appeal
to God—He always hears me.

"All I have to do is close my eyes,
bow my head with respect
and God hears my prayers up there in the sky,
And He doesn't mind if I don't genuflect!

"For He knows just what is in my heart, Dear.
And what I ask of Him each day
is to watch over my loved ones down here.
So you see, I don't have to kneel to pray!"

We Can't Forget Lena

By Pearl R. Tolzman

*T*first met Lena when I was 9 years old. I was standing on a corner with my father, waiting for a streetcar. Next to us was a short, rotund lady of middle years, wearing a white dress and a little white bonnet, and carrying in her hand what looked like a bunch of advertisements. Just as the car came, she smilingly handed us each one of her leaflets.

When we had paid our fare, we took our seats and commenced to read and found that the pamphlets were of a religious nature. The lady with the contagious smile happened to sit by me, and she was so friendly that I confided to her that my mother had recently died. She patted my cheek and said, "I must live near you. Come and see me any time you are lonely." She gave me her address, which proved to be only a few blocks from my home.

So it was that my friendship began with one of the most remarkable women I have ever chanced to meet. The following Saturday I walked by her house with my sister, and there was that beautiful lady, out sprinkling her lawn. She greeted me with so much love. Dropping the hose, shutting off the stream of water, she bid us come in, and out came a plate of big, round sugar cookies. When we had finished the plate of delicious sweets, she took out her guitar and played us the sweetest tunes. But sweetest of all was her lovely voice as she sang to us.

Lena had a heart as big as the world and it seemed to embrace everyone in it.

When it was time to go, my sister questioned, "What shall we call you?"

The answer came back quietly: "Lena."

Now, Lena had a heart as big as the world and it seemed to embrace everyone in it. My sister, Vi, and I made many excuses to venture past her house on the way home from school, and it got so that Lena would watch for us and beckon us from her kitchen window to come in, an invitation we never refused. Once in, there was always a plate of cookies, a glass of milk, or perhaps a coffee cake fresh out of the oven, and always she would sing to us, accompanied by the strumming of her guitar.

As we spent more time with Lena, we realized that by no means were we the only beneficiaries of her kindly nature. Lena trusted everyone. In those days, door-to-door agents were plentiful, and whether

Lena bought from them or not, they never left without a cup of her coffee and some of her home-baked goods. There was a fruit peddler by the name of George who came by once a week, and he was always asked to come in, sit down, and have some coffee and cake. He always gladly accepted, for no one ever tasted better coffee than our Swedish friend, Lena, made.

She never boiled her coffee. She bought the whole beans, ground them herself, measured just the right amount into a scalded white porcelain pitcher, poured boiling water over the grounds, let it steep a few minutes tightly covered, and there was a beverage fit for the gods. Hers was the first coffee I ever tasted, and although I started drinking it when I was just a child, it never seemed to hurt me any. Maybe it was the thick whipping cream she poured into it—I don't know—but no one has ever made coffee like Lena.

One day we girls insisted on bringing father over with us to see Lena and to meet her husband who was employed by the city transit company. He was a very quiet man, and their children had grown and moved away, but Lena never seemed to be lonely, as a steady stream of people seemed to come and go throughout the day.

When she found out that my father was a minister, she was very happy. She was devoutly religious, and she would go along on Saturdays with my father and us to visit the General Hospital wards, the Hopkins Poorhouse and the prisons. Wherever she went she spread a ray of sunshine, and I am sure the glow remained for some time after her departure.

In those days the middle 1920s, girls wore their hair in long braids. But my red mop was so thick that I had trouble getting the comb through it, resulting in a horrible, matted mess of tangles. It was Lena who had the patience and gentle, deft fingers to untangle what was almost an impossible jungle.

Lena was an expert cook, and the odd thing about her cooking was that it continued all day when she was home. Meals were never on time; if someone dropped in during the early afternoon, they would certainly be treated to a big meal as though it were 12 noon or 6 o'clock in the evening. One of her specialties was what she called veal kallops. It was a dish of Swedish origin, and the memory of it makes my mouth water. She cut the veal in cubes, browned them evenly, added salt and pepper, a wee bit of grated onion and a little mace, simmered the meat just covered with water until tender, and thickened the juice with a mixture of flour and water. She served it over a mound of rice, and it was scrumptious. I also remember her homemade bread and rolls and the butter drizzling over them, the lamb stew spiced with dill, and the rows and rows of her raspberry sauce, which was my favorite, and her jams and jellies.

Many a time when we girls were down with a bad cold, Lena would come walking down the path to our house, her arms laden with a jar of homemade chicken soup and a bowl of custard. She never seemed to get sick. If anyone in the neighborhood needed food or help, Lena supplied it. Her generosity, in spite of her not being wealthy by any means, caused some to ask, "How can you afford to be so generous?"

Her reply was always the same. "My God supplies my every need; I have never given away one apple but I got two back," she said.

Once someone told her about an old fellow who had become senile and was hospitalized. He was very unhappy, and Lena brought the old man into her home to care for him. Her husband objected, but to no avail; he quickly found that objecting to Lena's generosity and charity was like bucking against the wind, and he finally became used to it.

Once, when we were going out to our lake cabin, we did not to take our pet cat along, and Lena offered to care for it. At the end of the summer we found Kitty fat and glossy, but spoiled rotten and unwilling to drink the milk we offered her. When we asked Lena what she had fed her that made her so persnickety, she replied, "Oh, I gave her cream to drink and the best grade of red sockeye salmon." It took awhile to get Kitty unspoiled.

But it was not the food for our bodies that made a lasting impression on me as a child and as I grew up. It was Lena's kind heart, her smile, her comforting arms around me, her songs, her faith in God. She put something into my life that has lingered there, although it is now many a year since Lena walked down the path to our little motherless home. ❖

Plant Happiness

First, plant five rows of "peas":
Prayer,
Perseverance,
Politeness,
Promptness,
Purity.

Next plant three rows of "squash":
Squash gossip,
Squash criticism,
Squash indifference.

Then five rows of "lettuce":
Let us be faithful to duty,
Let us be unselfish,
Let us be truthful,
Let us follow Christ,
Let us love one another.

No garden is complete without "turnips":
Turn up for church,
Turn up with a smile,
Turn up with new ideas,
Turn up with determination to make everything count for something good and worthwhile.
Amen.

—Submitted by Grace V. Dove

Old Bill

By Len Colp

I had been in Vietnam about a year when Mom's letter came.

Dear Ben,

This is just a quick note. I thought that I should let you know that Old Bill died last Saturday. They buried him today.

I went to the funeral because he had been so good to you and I knew that you would want me to. Some of the others from the church were there as well.

There wasn't any of his family there. I guess you knew that Mrs. Lane died last year. When she was so ill, one of her daughters came and nursed her. It is said that when he was ill, they refused to come.

Bill had been ill six months with cancer. He often talked about his kids. They say they are well off and living in the East.

Well, I have to run, for your dad is waiting to mail this note. He is always in such a hurry since he retired.

Love,

Mom

I stretched out on my bunk and a tear or two rolled down my cheeks. Old Bill was dead. Old Bill was gone to the heaven he talked about so much.

My mind rolled back the years to the days when I was 12 or so. Dad was busy trucking then. He was never home much and I missed him a lot.

Old Bill moved into our area and began coming to our church. "A retired farmer," they said. "A new convert to the faith," they gossiped.

He saw a lonely boy whose father was never home and stepped in to fill the vacant spot. "Let's go fishin', Ben," he'd say, and fishin' we'd go, come Saturday morning.

After a couple of hours fishing off the old creek bank, he'd say, "Let's give the fish a break." We hadn't caught a thing. "Let's just have a little talk with Jesus."

Right then, on the banks of the old Ribstone Creek, we'd bow our heads and he'd begin to talk to God. He didn't pray. He just talked to God.

"God," he'd say, "you see us here on the banks of the old Ribby. God, you know we'd like a fish or two just so we can prove we've been a-fishin'. Any size will do, Lord.

"God, you know the troubles in this old world. You know I ain't complaining, for you've been so good to me. I just want to remind you about my family.

"There's Thelma and her family, Lord. I didn't show her right and now she's too old for me to make her listen. God, maybe she'll hear You.

"Remember Nor-Ann. Lord, if I had only lived for you 40 years ago, things might be different now."

By now his voice was quivering and tears were running down the rough old face that was marred by drink and sin. It always seemed to me he kind of forgot me at times like that.

"Lord," he'd say in a breaking voice, "Lord, save them from the wickedness of my ways, the ways I taught them.

"Don't You dare forget about Hugh, God. You know what I dragged that boy through—the times in a drunken stupor I beat him within an inch of his life. Lord, don't forget him. I know it's a little late to be expecting him to love me, but Lord, save his soul from hell. That's all I ask.

"God, there's Billy Boy. God, if it is possible, take my life for his. I taught him to curse, to drink and take everything he could get without

> *He saw a lonely boy and stepped in to fill the vacant spot. "Let's go fishin', Ben," he'd say, and fishin' we'd go.*

offering anything in return. It's not his fault, Lord; it's mine."

Sometimes I wondered if he remembered that I was there as he talked away to God, just like God was sitting on the grass beside us. I would open my eyes to see if maybe God hadn't just taken on human form.

When Old Bill had finished praying, he'd say to me, "Ben, you talk to God." I'd try to pray like him, try to talk to God, but my prayers were always just prayers.

When our little prayer meeting was over, we'd cast our lines back into the brownish water again. It always seemed that the sun shone a little brighter, the meadow flowers bloomed a little prettier, and the birds sang a little sweeter after Old Bill had talked to God. And often as not, we would get that fish or two.

As I grew older, I heard the stories of his life. Some, I suppose, was idle gossip, but others told it like it was.

A young boy born in eastern Canada, Bill had had a praying mother who took him to church every Sunday, morning and night. She had believed in family prayer meetings. In spite of all her prayers and teaching, Old Bill forsook her path. His mother never ceased to pray for him. In fact, it was said that when she knew she was dying, she asked the family who would pray for Bill after she was gone. There was a sister who promised to carry on.

He married a girl and there never was another like her. If there had ever been a saint, it was Ann. He took her on a train to the West when women seldom made the trip. He dropped her on the homestead. She knew what it was to put the crop in and be six months pregnant. She knew what it was to have to defend that child from a drunken, raving, cursing man. She had felt his blows. And he never fooled her; she knew that he spent many a night with some cheap beauty in the area.

But there was nothing modern about her, and divorce never entered her mind. She was Old Bill's wife and she had vowed to live with him until death parted them.

When our little prayer meeting was over, we'd cast our lines back into the brownish water again.

He worked the local ranches to get money enough to buy liquor. He'd come home with a week's wages in his pocket, but he had no intentions of giving her a nickel. How she fed his kids was her business. She was forced to steal money from his pockets while he slept to buy Hugh a pair of shoes for school. While he slept, she played Robin Hood so that she could buy enough groceries to see them through.

It was her skimping that gave her daughters the schooling that made them RN's. Her determination gave her sons a trade. And when the kids fled the farm, they said, "Come, Mom, leave him to his drink and devilish ways."

"No," she replied, "Billy needs me."

At 65, Old Bill was mulling through the years of keepsakes the family had collected. Up in the corner of the attic he found his mother's Bible. It had been there ever since he had built the house. He wiped the dust off its covers and began to read. He hadn't read anything like that since he was a boy in Sunday school. "For all have sinned and come short of the glory of God." No one needed to tell Old Bill that, nor did they need to tell him, "For the wages of sin is death."

Then he read, "For God so loved the world that He gave His only begotten Son, that whosoever believeth in Him should not perish but have everlasting life." He remembered hearing that verse quoted differently and more personally and it came back to his groggy mind. "For God so loved Old Bill that He gave His only begotten Son that if Old Bill believed in Him, Old Bill should not perish but have everlasting life."

The next few days he thought long and hard about it and he found it very difficult to put the Bible down.

One cold December evening, down in the old log cow barn, it seemed that God said to him, "It's now or never."

"Now or never!" He got up from the milk stool, hung the pail up on the peg, dropped onto his knees in the hay and began to pray.

When the chores were done, he went to the

house. His wife knew before he told her that Old Bill was a New Bill.

After they retired, people sometimes complained about some of his rough corners, for he never was a model gentleman. But his wife would smile and say, "God knows all about Billy."

He began to tell what God had done for him. Like one neighbor said, "If you knew Bill before and after, he didn't need to tell you that he had become a Christian." Old Bill was as different as St. Paul was different from Saul.

The sad part of it was that his kids remembered only the Bill of their childhood, the Bill who had beat them, the Bill who had starved them. They seemed unable to allow themselves

to see the difference. He tried hard to earn their love and respect—I don't suppose any man tried harder—but the damage was done.

The night that God reached down and took Ann, he cried like a baby. He had hoped for more years to make up for the years of heartache he had caused her.

Well, now he is with her. Sometimes, I wish that I could meet his kids and tell them of the times on the banks of the Old Ribby, when I heard him talk to God about them—pleading for them and offering, if it were possible, to go to hell for them.

I have never met them, but I thank God from the bottom of my heart that I heard Old Bill talk to God. ❖

Bottom of the Matter

By Robert G. Tucker

*I*n June 1945, the German high command had just surrendered in Europe; the imperial Japanese forces would throw in the towel before the summer was over; and the Rev. Orrin B. Snum's annual strawberry festival was demolished by a minor blitzkrieg.

My tag-along 10-year-old brother, Rusty, and my best pal, Tom Cheever, and I couldn't take any credit for the Axis armies' losing ways, but we sure masterminded the bombardment of the poor preacher's ill-fated strawberry fete. Tom was 13 that summer, and I was about a year younger.

Our plan was a masterpiece of simplicity. Half a package of Fourth of July cherry bombs, bought with pooled allowance money, were Scotch-taped together with their fuses wrapped about the base of a smoldering Old Gold cigarette. (While Tom's dad was off fighting the Japanese in the Pacific, Tom would occasionally liberate a forbidden "coffin nail" from his mother's purse.)

If the planning had been masterful, the execution of the diabolic plot was a work of pure genius. The "T-Bomb" (named in honor to Tom, who thought up the idea) was lighted and placed under a crepe-festooned table on the lawn of the Methodist Church while the congregation was inside singing Gospel hymns.

When the cherry bombs exploded at the church social, Pa knew how to get to the bottom of the dad-dratted matter.

The delayed fuse gave us about a quarter of an hour to establish our alibis, and we took advantage of the time by going inside to be seen mingling innocently with the crowd. The grown-ups were wearing their best Sunday-go-to meeting outfits. The girls wore white print dresses trimmed in pink; we boys had donned crisp white ducks, starched white shirts and strawberry-pink neckties for the occasion.

The hymn-sing over, the lighthearted crowd adjourned to the church lawn where refreshments were spread out on the table directly over the ominously smoking cigarette fuse. Old Preacher Snum, roly-poly and unctuous as always, offered up a prayer for God's blessing upon the food and was about to cut into a huge strawberry chiffon cake when the T-Bomb went off—not with a single bang, but with a staccato series of explosions that sounded as if the strawberry festival was being strafed by a Messerschmitt ME-109. And from the crowd's reaction, you would have sworn that a rogue Luftwaffe pilot was taking out his frustration on the Methodists of Hampton Falls, N.H. People screamed and ran. The refreshment table collapsed, dumping the beautiful strawberry chiffon cake and a huge bowl of strawberry punch onto the grass. The deacons, dour Wesleyans all, ran about like frantic squirrels, trying vainly to identify the perpetrators of the horrendous deed.

They came up with several possibilities, including boys from the

Congregational Church across the town common, but Tom and Rusty and I were not among the suspects. We had pulled off the perfect crime. Or so we thought.

Tom Cheever and his mother ate dinner at our house that evening. After the meal, we all gathered around the venerable Emerson radio in the parlor to listen to the madcap adventures of the irrepressible Blondie and her long-suffering husband, Dagwood. That was when my dog, a cocker spaniel named Prince, chose to amble in and drop a love offering between my feet for all to see. Prince's "gift" was the unused half-package of Thunderclap cherry bombs that I had carefully hidden under my bed. The jig was up and we all knew it.

Pa sighed long and loudly. "So, that's how it is," he said. Then he arose, clicked the radio off and left the room. He returned after a moment, snapping a well-oiled razor strop against his right thigh. "Robbie, Rusty," he commanded, "we'll step out back to the woodshed, boys, where I'm fixing to get straight to the bottom of this dad-dratted matter."

Mrs. Cheever looked helplessly up at my father. "Oh, Dan," she said, "I'm not strong enough. Would you mind terribly?"

"Not at all, Alice. Fall in, Tom. You're included, too."

Feet dragging, we three miscreants began our march to the woodshed. As I filed past Ma, I cast a slyly angelic smile at her, but received only a frown of disapproval in return.

"Take your pants off, guys," Pa said firmly, closing the woodshed door behind him and snapping on a flyspecked light bulb that dangled from the ceiling at the end of a frayed cord.

"Aw, Pa, we was only funnin'," my little brother asserted lamely.

"Is that a fact?" Pa stopped to help Rusty with his belt buckle, my brother's fingers having turned to rubber. " This will remind you to set some limits on your funnin' the next time. You and I have been through this before, boy. You know what to do."

"Yes, sir," my brother sighed miserably. After hanging his white ducks on a nail, he

moved a straight-backed wooden chair, kept for just such occasions, to the middle of the floor and jackknifed indecorously over the backrest, making a target of his puckered behind. "Pa, you're humiliatin' us," my little brother complained dolefully.

"Hold still, boy," our pa replied, and he proceeded to lay on seven vigorous spanks to the accompaniment of wall-shaking yowls of protest from Rusty.

And then Tom was bending over the chair and Pa was hoisting his shirttails. I leaned back against the woodshed wall and shook as my boyhood buddy got peppered 10 times by Pa's ferocious strop. Then, while Tom Cheever was whooping in anguish and doing his own fair imitation of a Comanche war dance, my father beckoned for me to present myself.

The refreshment table collapsed, dumping the beautiful strawberry chiffon cake and a huge bowl of strawberry punch onto the grass.

I approached the chair as if I was walking on eggshells. My bottom itched as I could smell Neat's foot oil on Pa's razor strop. Grimly, I bent over the backrest and lifted my shirttails. Silver teardrops glistened on the seat of the chair.

"Son, this will hurt me more 'n it hurts you," my pa assured me.

"I doubt it, sir," I answered honestly, gritting my teeth and screwing up my face muscles.

The licking was administered quickly and it felt as if a swarm of angry yellow jackets was attacking my bare fundament. When Pa was finished, even Rusty and Tom stopped yowling to stare at me in awe and cover their ears to block out my lusty caterwauling.

That all happened nearly 55 years ago. Between our tail-whuppin's and having to get up in front of the congregation to apologize for our behavior the following Sunday, we three small, overly exuberant boys were miraculously toned down.

Nowadays, of course, the juvenile court would become involved, along with a passel of social workers and child psychiatrists, each one trying to analyze our patterns of repressed hostility. Pa's gone now, but if he were around, he could sure tell the experts how to get to the seat of a boy's behavior problem! ❖

The Eighth Amen

By Henry Chequer, Jr.

The other day I ran into Percy. "Have you sung any amens lately?" I asked. Every time I meet Percy, I ask him the same question. Percy never answers, and gets an expression on his face as if to say he wishes I'd forget the whole thing.

Years ago we were choirboys together in a small church not far away. Beginners in the choir were paid 5 cents a week, but in a few months, when promoted to chorister, the pay was increased to 15 cents a week. By today's standards it wasn't very much, but we considered ourselves fortunate to be able to bring home even so small an amount.

All our choir rehearsals and efforts were pointed to singing the Sunday services to the satisfaction of the choirmaster. It was the custom to conclude the services with a sung amen. We knew a number of amens from which the choirmaster could select: a few single amens, a couple of twofold amens, one or two threefold amens and even a sevenfold amen.

The choirmaster wished to add a new dimension, and wrote an eightfold amen. We practiced it week after week to the point of wishing that grown-ups wouldn't get inspirations about writing new amens. In his eightfold amen, the first amen was sung quietly; the second a little louder, each amen louder than the last, until the eighth amen.

Before this final amen, the choirmaster had written "lunga" to show that no ordinary breath would do but that we were to take a real deep breath. In addition, the eighth amen was noted with three F's—not two for double forte or fortissimo, but three for triple forte or fortissi-issi-mo. As if that weren't sufficient, he had written above the last amen, "Give Forth Lustily."

After Percy had left the choir room the choirmaster told the choir that he had decided, after all, to omit the last amen from his eightfold amen.

We practiced this small masterpiece over and over, week after week, and finally the day arrived. But a few minutes before the church service, it was noticed that the organ boy, whose job it was to pump the organ, hadn't shown up. Possibly because Percy's voice was changing—or maybe it was because he was standing closest to the choirmaster—that the choirmaster pointed to him and said, "You pump the organ."

There wasn't time for Percy to put his music away, so he took it with him, crossed the chancel to the organ and squeezed through the narrow door by the organ bench. He went through the narrow passage, by the connections from the keyboard and stops to the pipes, and into the small area in back of the organ where the pump handle projected from the bellows. Pumping the handle forced air into the large bellows, which in turn provided compressed air to the pipes.

After Percy had left the choir room (the organ boy always preceded the organist so as to have time to fill the bellows with air before the organist arrived), the choirmaster told the choir that he had decided, after all, to omit the last amen from his eightfold amen.

You can probably guess what happened, but I'll tell you anyway. We could hear Percy singing along with us most of the time; he had a complete set of the music for the service. The service drew to a close. It was time for the eightfold amen. We sang the first amen softly, and the second, the third, each more loudly than the last. We could hear Percy joining in. We sang the seventh amen, and stopped.

From behind the organ came the eighth amen sung by Percy, floating on the air like the wail of a banshee—with adenoids—and "given forth lustily," as the music had said.

When we came into the choir room, the boys broke up in hysterics. After awhile, Percy appeared, his arms akimbo as if to ask, "What happened?" The choirmaster already had left in a hurry, and one or two who saw him said he had a funny look on his face.

We posted Percy on the bulletin board as the "Boy of the Month," although there were some who felt he hadn't earned the honor. It was the last time we had an eightfold amen—and it was the last time Percy was asked to pump the organ. ❖

He Wasn't Religious

By Edna N. Sutherland

They said he wasn't religious. True, he didn't believe in going to church, although he worked as hard and as long as anyone to get our first church built. If people would apply as much thought and energy to helping their fellowman in everyday living, he often said, as they did in getting ready for and going to church, the world would be a lot better place—and he lived his beliefs.

His friends and neighbors respected him, and often sought his wise counsel, but they always said he wasn't religious. They said it as if that were the thing that mattered.

I am his daughter, and I knew him as one who loved his fellowman—a most religious man.

He didn't go to the welcoming parties that were commonly given for a newly arrived homesteader. His wife, my mother, always went and took her cakes and cookies and any article that she could spare to help the new family get settled in.

After the novelty of having another new member added to our small community of pioneers had worn off, my dad would slowly walk the bush trails to the homesteader's cabin.

In a quiet voice, my father would introduce himself to the newcomer, and say, "Well, Neighbor, I see you have a family of little ones. They can't get along without milk, you know. I hear you've got no cow. I'll be sending over a pail of milk every day as long as you need it. Thanks aren't required, but I expect you to do the same for the next man, should he need it."

Another homestead, another family: aunts, uncles, cousins, sons, daughters-in-law, children and grandchildren. Many mouths, but no garden. Another trek across the meadow and over the ridge. Another introduction to another new settler.

"Glad to know you, Neighbor. See you have a big family. No land broken yet, I hear. I laid out the bit of land, an acre or two, at the foot of my field near to your quarter. Put in a garden and some spuds and you'll be all set for winter. Cut a trail through my stand of poplar, if you will; make it a lot easier to get into the garden. Cut up the poplar and use it this winter. Need all the wood we can get. It gets mighty cold here."

No mention of the work to break and ready this "bit of land." No mention that every inch of land was as precious as gold, or more, to the settler. Just do the same for the next guy who needs it.

Milk for the family to the west, garden for the ones to the north, a lift into town—40 miles away—for someone else. A big family dinner for the ill-equipped homesteader with the near-starving family. A night sitting up to save a precious cow with milk fever. The loan of a horse to another who would never be able to return the favor. Nothing much in any one case, but a constant, kindly, humble help to all "down on their luck." He always was there to give "just a little help along the way," like a neighborly chat over a cup of coffee with a man needing assurance that he had indeed done the right thing by bringing his family to help open up the country.

They said he wasn't religious, but he loved man and beast. He loved the brilliant hues of a fiery red sunset. He could watch the fleecy summer clouds floating in a sea of blue for hours, until tasks of greater importance called him away. The dark, somber green of the spruce and pine, the airy, pastel greens of the poplar and birch brought peace and quiet to his life on busy, work-worn days. When he worked in the bush, cutting wood for the winter, he would gaze in awe at the cathedral-like bower of towering pines; he should listen reverently to the great silence heard only in the deepest woods.

They said he wasn't religious, but I never heard him raise his voice in anger to man or child or beast. I never saw him harm the lowliest creature. He said that every creature, no matter how humble, had its own place in the scheme of things. No insect or bug was without its place in creation. There was wonder in the little green sprout emerging from the moist brown earth covering a little dried seed. All God's creatures had as much right to life as any of us, we were taught. A reverence for all life has followed his children through theirs.

Pets, animals or wild things were never to be harmed in any way. Their needs were to be met before our own. They could not speak; therefore, their needs must be anticipated and met. Any dumb animal must be fed before you fed yourself. They must be protected as one would protect the small and innocent.

No, he didn't go to church. They often said that he wasn't religious.

Could we but measure up, in our day and age, to the standards of an unlettered man who loved God. May I be as religious as my father! ❖

A Small Boy & His Father's Prayers

By Mrs. L.W. Hall

When Father prays, he doesn't use
The words the preacher does;
There's different things for different days
But mostly it's for us.

When Father prays, the house is still—
His voice is slow and deep.
We shut our eyes, the clock ticks loud,
So quiet we must keep.

He prays that we may be good boys,
And later on, good men;
And then we squirm and think we won't
Have any quarrels again.

You'd never think to look at Dad
He once had tempers, too.
I guess, if Father needs to pray,
We youngsters surely do.

Sometimes the prayer gets very long
And hard to understand,
And then I wiggle up quite close
And let him hold my hand.

I can't remember all of it—
I'm little yet, you see;
But this one thing I can't forget—
My father prays for me!

The Christmas Grandfather Remembered Most

By Nova M. Lee

When Grandfather said, "Now I recollect when I was a lad," his grandchildren gathered around. In us he had an attentive audience and nothing could have pleased him more.

In summer he told about the "old swimming hole" and haying season. But in December he always told us winter stories, mostly about Christmas and how they celebrated when he was a boy and after he and Grandmother had a family of their own.

"That little church," he began his favorite account, "set right in the middle of the woods; tall cedars they were mostly." He had our interest.

"Yes, I can still see that little church." Often he would pause as though drifting back through the years and one of us would prompt, "Go on, Grandfather."

> *"We never missed a Sunday going to church. Sometimes the ground would be covered with snow, but we just bundled up and piled into the sleigh."*

He would smile, then continue. "We never missed a Sunday going to church. Sometimes the ground would be frozen or covered with snow, but this did not stop us. We just bundled up and piled into the sleigh."

The story was not new to us, but we never tired of hearing it. There were three houses, we knew, near the church. The "parson" and his family lived in one; Mr. Grover, who taught the school, lived in the other, and the small house was occupied by old Ben.

"He had no family of his own," Grandfather said, "but he loved all the people in the valley."

Old Ben was a hard worker, even though he had a lame leg and walked with a limp. He did odd jobs for the parson and Mr. Grover, "everything from tending vegetable gardens in summer to cutting wood and shoveling snow in winter," Grandfather said.

He was a kind, gentle man, giving much of himself and asking little or nothing in return. He was honest and trustworthy and the people depended heavily upon him. "Someone was always taking their problems to old Ben," Grandfather said. "And he never failed them. I've

seen him tackle that problem like he would a big load of wood."

The Christmas Grandfather remembered most was the year Mr. Tyler fell off the barn (he was putting on a new roof) and was "laid up for quite a spell," according to Grandfather. Mr. Tyler, it seemed, was the valley's dependable Santa for the church Christmas tree.

So they were faced with finding someone to take his place. The parson could not, for he had to give the prayer and lead the singing. Mr. Grover had a voice every kid in the valley would recognize, no matter how hard he tried to disguise it.

The next runner-up was Grandfather, and he came down with a case of laryngitis. "I could hardly speak above a whisper," he said.

So what were they going to do? Mr. Jordan was so skinny it would take all the feather pillows in the valley to fatten him up. Mr. Emery was so fat he would have trouble getting through the door; Mr. Jameson had poor eyesight.

"Well," said Mrs. Benson (she had her nose stuck into everything, according to Grandfather), "if we don't have anyone to play Santa, I don't think we should have a tree."

"Oh, the children would be too disappointed," Grandmother said.

"If there is no one else," Mrs. Sims said, "I'll ask George to be Santa."

George would have made the worst kind of Santa and everyone knew it, including Mrs. Sims. He was a shy, timid little man with a lisp to his speech.

As the days went on, the people became more and more worried. Mr. Tyler was not improving and Grandfather's laryngitis hung on. "I was as squeaky as a mouse," he told us.

When they met at the church on Christmas Eve to trim the big cedar, anxiety hung heavy. There was not a single prospect to wear the red suit with fur trim. They had gone over the list of men in the valley a dozen times, but no one had the answer.

Often he would pause as though drifting back through the years and one of us would prompt, "Go on, Grandfather."

"When we went home for supper and to fetch the children, we didn't know what was going to happen." Grandfather smiled as only he could. "We tried hard to keep those little fellows from knowing anything was wrong, so I took the older boys with me to do the chores, and Ellen (that was Grandmother) and Lucy went to the kitchen." He slapped his knee. "What a supper Ellen would cook up! We had vegetable stew, baked yams, hot biscuits and milk, topped off with pumpkin pie."

He paused before he said, "I don't know why the young'uns didn't catch on that something was not right, for Ellen was as nervous as a cat and I kept bathing my chest with liniment. Finally Ellen said, 'It's no use, William,' and she was right."

Anyway, they put on their warmest clothes and Grandfather brought the sleigh up to the gate. "Ellen put a hot brick wrapped in an old blanket on the floor to keep the children's feet warm on the way," he said. "As we drove away, a few snowflakes began to fall, and I told Ellen we'd better start home as soon as the gifts had been handed out, for the snow might get heavy." Grandfather gave a short chuckle. "And being a woman who worried a lot, Ellen sighed. She was thinking there would be no Santa to hand out the gifts."

The church was crowded and the children were excited. Old Ben had outdone himself, cleaning and trimming the kerosene lamps. Their quivering light caught the popcorn strings on the tree. "It looked like the snowflakes had come in and settled on that cedar," Grandfather said.

Every family had kept the secret from the children, who sat with their eyes as bright as the candles on the tree, Grandfather said. But the mothers and fathers sat straight in their seats, wondering who was going to break the news that Santa would not be there.

Mr. Jordan leaned over and whispered to Grandfather, "William, what are they going to do about you know what? They'd better take me up."

Grandfather just shook his head and said

nothing. "Ellen was looking pale and more worried all the time," he said. "And so were the other mothers."

"We had a lot of anxious moments," Grandfather said. "I kept trying to force my voice and spoke to Ellen a few times, but I was as wheezy as ever."

Mrs. Sims spoke to George and the poor fellow crouched down in his seat as far as he could get. "George Sims wasn't hankering for that job," Grandfather said.

The older children put on a short program. "But I don't think many of us heard a word," he said. "We kept thinking how disappointed the children were going to be."

Then the parson got up and said, "I know the children have all been waiting for this moment, so we won't delay any longer. I think Santa has arrived."

There was the sound of bells outside, then the door opened—and there was Santa! Everyone turned and looked to see who was missing from the crowd, but they were all there. Not one man of the valley had slipped out.

Santa waved, tossed kisses toward the children and gave out with a healthy, "Ho! Ho! Merry Christmas!" He kept waving to the children and laughing in the jolliest way as he went over to the tree. He looked it up and down and said. "My! My! You must have been good boys and girls this year. My sleigh was weighted down when I got here." He looked toward the children. "You see, I had to bring your toys by, then go on to visit some boys and girls who can't come to the church."

He began to take gifts from the tree; older boys and girls helped take them to the children. He would chuckle and nod and rub his fat stomach.

"No one knew who he was," Grandfather said, "but he was about the best Santa the valley had ever known. He sure made Mr. Tyler look bad."

All the time gifts were being distributed, the parents were wondering who was under that suit. They had never heard that voice before. If it was one of the valley people, he was doing a good job of disguising it.

"But no one was missing as far as we could tell," Grandfather said. "You know, it almost had me believing in Santa."

When the last gift had been taken from the tree, the jolly Santa waved and tossed kisses again. "Merry Christmas!" he called. "Enjoy your toys and be good boys and girls and I'll be back next year." He skipped across the stage, tossed more kisses, and was out the door.

The one thing the people had forgotten in their concern over Santa was to consult old Ben, but he had not neglected to work on the problem. Earlier that day, when he went into the woods to fetch a big log for the church stove, he saw a man cutting through the cedar breaks. Old Ben had called to him and the man stopped.

Right away Old Ben had known who the stranger was; it was not far from the water stop, and a hobo had left the train in hopes of finding a farmhouse where he could beg food and a place to sleep out of the snowy night. "Old Ben had a kind voice," Grandfather said, "and I guess that bum could tell he meant no harm."

After they had talked awhile, Ben made the tramp a proposition. He would give him all the food he could eat and a night's lodging if he would play the church Santa. "I can't bear to see those children disappointed," he told him.

Ben made the tramp a proposition. He would give him all the food he could eat and a night's lodging if he would play the church Santa.

"Well, now that hobo sure took him up," Grandfather chuckled. "I'll bet it was the first time he had been in a church since he was a lad and his Pa and Ma took him."

He went back to the house with old Ben, and while he was putting away three bowls of hot mush, a baked yam and coffee, Ben took his idea to the parson. "If it had been anybody except old Ben," Grandfather said, "that parson would have said 'No' right off. But he respected Ben and trusted him."

However, it seemed the parson did have some misgivings and suggested they go talk it over with Mr. Grover. Being a schoolteacher, Mr. Grover lacked the faith in people that the parson had, so he was a bit stubborn. "I don't like it," he said.

"But time is running out, Mr. Grover," the parson said.

"It's too risky," was Mr. Grover's argument. "I'll have no part of it."

"He won't give us any trouble." Old Ben spoke up for the first time.

"We can't be sure of that," Mr. Grover said, "He's a hobo, a tramp. I don't want a man like that handing out gifts to our children."

The parson and old Ben were silent.

"Why," said Mr. Grover, "he would probably eat the fruit and candy right off the tree."

"I don't think so," the parson said. "I don't think so at all."

"Well, no, Parson, if you want to give your consent, go right ahead. But I'll have nothing to do with it," Mr. Grover said.

"But think of the children," the parson said.

"Yes, do think of them," said Mr. Grover. "Receiving gifts from the hands of a tramp. The idea is ridiculous! Absolutely ridiculous."

"I don't agree." The parson was getting a little impatient with Mr. Grover's disagreeable manner.

"Then it's up to you," the teacher said.

The parson and old Ben walked back to his house. The parson was thoughtful, yet he did not see what they had to lose. The man would be dressed in Santa's suit and no one would know who he was until it was over. He felt a little smug. It just might be a good joke on Mrs. Benson.

"You feel he can be trusted, don't you, Ben?" he asked.

"I know he can, Parson," Ben answered. "I'll take the responsibility if anything happens, which it won't. But if it does, you can blame me."

The parson was silent.

"As soon as he hands out the presents, he will head for my kitchen where he will find more food waiting," Ben said. "You can take my word for it."

What more could the parson ask? "All right, Ben," he said. "We'll go ahead, but you don't have to take the responsibility. If anything happens, it is as much my fault as yours."

"Nothing is going to happen," Ben promised. "And I think he will make a right jolly Santa."

So, once more, by the love and generosity of an old man's heart, a problem was solved and the children were not denied a visit from Santa.

"Yes, we had a fine Christmas and a jolly Santa," Grandfather said. "And all because one lonely old man knew the real meaning of "goodwill toward men." ❖

The Surprising Story of Dorothy Bell

By Mary Boyd as told to Etta Lynch

In the early 1920s, my husband was appointed pastor to the Methodist church in Albany, Texas, a beautiful little town nestled in a valley surrounded by rolling green hills. In 1926, a Methodist minister's wife was accepted as an unpaid associate.

Predictably, I was asked to give the children of our parish some much-needed religious instruction. One Monday afternoon, the children were invited to gather to help organize a Junior Missionary Society. They came, loaded with pent-up energy, ready for almost anything but religious worship.

Before attempting to convert children who preferred roller-skating and running games, I directed a play period on the large grassy lawn of the church. After a short play period, the children filed into the Sunday-school classroom. They were ready to get acquainted with me and to test me, so I found myself unable to curb their restless wriggling. Realizing I must find a definite project to occupy their minds, I dismissed them and hurried home to search for material.

That evening, as I read the newspaper, my attention was drawn to a boxed message: The World Friendship for Children invited children's groups to join in sending a boatload of dolls from American children to the children of Japan. The idea seemed perfect for girls, but would the boys be interested?

Dorothy Bell Albany on the day of her farewell party in the United States.

The following Monday I found my little group had doubled. We played together first, then sang songs, and I presented a short Bible message. Finally, I presented the idea of showing our friendship to Japan by sending a doll to their children. The response of the children was amazing. Not only were they willing to participate, they were willing to contribute their allowances to buy the doll.

At the next meeting, the children brought their nickels and pennies. I bought the prettiest doll on the store's shelf. She was dressed in traveling clothes, neat dress, pretty hat, shoes and socks. When I presented my purchase to the class, she captured their hearts.

A mischievous boy raised his hand and darted from the room. In seconds he returned with a tiny chair from the nursery.

"This is just right for the doll to sit in," he said, his eyes bright. "Now, the doll needs a name." His interest quieted my uneasiness that the boys might not participate, and after a great deal of discussion, we named her Dorothy Bell Albany.

Through the reports of their children, parents became interested and many offered to help. Our project came to the attention of Lizzie Dodge, an expert seamstress who made most of the baby clothes in Albany. Handicapped from birth by lower limbs that hadn't developed, Miss Lizzie navigated by crawling. This determined lady presented our class with an exquisite wardrobe for Dorothy Bell.

The Junior Missionary Society at Albany, Texas, with Dorothy Bell (center, foreground) on the day of her departure for Japan. Photo courtesy of Mary Boyd, Austin, Texas.

Though I encouraged the children's participation in dressing the doll and procuring her passport, I placed the greatest emphasis on the fact that our doll was a symbol of love and friendship toward the children of Japan.

"If we grow up always thinking of foreign people with love," I told them earnestly, "war will be impossible."

As the day of Dorothy's departure neared, the children planned a farewell party. Parents brought ice cream and cake, expressing gratitude that their offspring had become involved in a project of love. Since the children had become attached to Dorothy Bell, I waited until all had gone home before I wrapped the doll for her overseas journey. She joined 13,000 other little messengers of peace.

In the weeks that followed, the children asked often, "Have you had a letter from any of the Japanese children yet?" And time after time, I had to disappoint them.

But one morning, the mail contained an unusual round package with a strange return address—from Japan. Eagerly I opened it and found beautiful hand-painted pictures. Before the next meeting, I sent word to all that we had heard from the Japanese children, and all the children came to see the pictures.

"The colors are beautiful!" one little girl

exclaimed. "They look like crayon colors, but they're a lot brighter."

The children took turns sharing the pictures with their public school classmates and teachers, and the friendship idea expanded.

Time flew by, and the delightful experience slipped into my past. Tension grew between nations, and soon America was at war with Japan. I wondered if I had underestimated the value of building world friendship.

In 1943, Japanese military authorities ordered all of the friendship dolls destroyed. They were removed from honored niches, pierced or smashed with bamboo spears, doused with gasoline and set afire. But a few defied the order and hid the dolls away.

Twenty-eight years passed, and I celebrated my 80th birthday. One afternoon the phone rang, and a strange woman spoke to me.

"Mrs. Boyd? This is Elsa Turner, social editor of The Albany News. Do you remember mailing a doll to Japan back in 1926, as a friendship gesture to Japanese children?"

"I remember it well. Why?"

Elsa Turner's explanation answered the question that had haunted me for over half a century. Had our long-ago gesture of friendship been a waste? Had it accomplished anything? The answer was a heartening "Yes!"

From Mrs. Turner I learned the story: In March of 1978, a Japanese reporter received a tip that a mysterious and very old doll had been discovered in a closet at Takedate Primary School in Aomori, Japan. Stored along with the doll was a passport, written in both Japanese and English, with American and Japanese flags stamped on it. The paper had yellowed and cracked with age, but the writing was clear.

Along with the passport was the letter I'd written to the Japanese children. Intrigued, the reporter, Masahiko Kohno, sent a copy of the passport, the letter and two color photos of the doll to the newspaper in Albany, Texas. His letter asked for the history behind the dolls—especially who had sponsored the idea and what they had hoped to accomplish.

Not long after the call from Elsa Turner, I received a letter from Mr. Kohno. "When Dorothy was found, I wrote a story for our evening news show," wrote the correspondent for the Aomori Bureau of Japan Broadcasting Corporation. "Also, the story was broadcast on our nationwide network. We had quite a good response from our audience. The story warmed the hearts of the people here. We had many letters and calls from people who remembered the friendship dolls."

Kohno had included two color photos of the doll, and I hurried to my souvenir collection to compare them to my own black-and-white photo. Indeed, the recently discovered doll was Dorothy Bell Albany. Once more, I returned to the letter from Masahiko Kohno.

"Schoolchildren at Takedate Primary School were surprised and excited to find Dorothy was a special gift sent by your Albany people to the children of Japan more than 50 years ago," he wrote. "She is now a treasure in the school. Against your goodwill, we had a war, but Dorothy is really a friendship doll, even after these many years. She shows children how it is important to love, not to hate."

Alone in my apartment, I smiled. After 50 years, I knew that our gesture of friendship had paid dividends. Thirteen thousand dolls had been shipped, and one doll was given to each school. Each child had been touched by the message that American children loved them and desired peace between their nations. Our gesture of friendship had spread like ripples from a rock, dropped into a pool of water, creating ever-widening circles that touch more lives than anyone will ever know. ❖

Top: Dorothy Bell, wearing one of the hand-crocheted dresses in her extensive wardrobe.
Middle: A more recent close-up of Dorothy Bell.
Above: The Takedate Primary School in Aomori, Japan, where Dorothy Bell was found.
Photos courtesy of Masahiko Kohno, staff correspondent, Aomori Bureau of
Japan Broadcasting Corporation.

God Is My Landlord

By William Engle
Reprinted from American Weekly, *1949*
Submitted by Martha Woodward,
Perry Hayden's daughter

*I*n the lead was the Quaker miller, Perry Hayden. With him were 12 boys. Gravely they walked down a street in the town of Tecumseh, Mich., out into the open country, and in the corner of a field in the autumn sunshine, they prepared to plant the world's strangest wheat crop.

They spaded and leveled a plot 4 feet by 8 feet, and the boys sowed a cubic inch of wheat—360 kernels—in 12 little rows.

It was the afternoon of September 26, 1940, and it marked the beginning of an experiment that today has worldwide significance.

"Bless this sowing, Lord, and make Thy face to shine upon it," the Midwest miller prayed, and he promised to give a 10th, or a tithe, of the harvest to the Lord's work.

He promised to sow the remaining 9/10, and from the second harvest give back a 10th—and so on for six years.

The Lord did bless that sowing, and His face shone upon that little corner of Michigan.

In the sixth year, the wheat field that had been 4 feet by 8 feet grew to 2,666 acres.

The harvest that year was a golden, wheaten mountain—72,150 bushels of the finest Bald Rock soft red winter wheat that ever came out of the earth.

The urge to try the wheat-tithing experiment came to him in the text of a sermon preached one day by a Cleveland Bible College student.

The six years of tithing, with the successive crops multiplying vastly, dramatized as nothing had before the old and hallowed tithing principle. Color motion pictures were made of each year's harvesting. These today are being shown up and down the country, and Perry Hayden, the Tecumseh miller, is giving almost all his time to the work of spreading the tithing idea across the land.

The urge to try the wheat-tithing experiment came to him in the text of a sermon preached one day by a Cleveland Bible College student, Clifton J. Robinson, in the Tecumseh Friends Church. It was John 12:24, and it ran:

"Verily, verily I say unto you, except a corn (kernel) of wheat fall into the ground and die, it abideth along; but if it die, it bringeth forth much fruit."

He decided to plant a kernel of wheat; then changed the plan to provide the first planting be a cubic inch; and he asked Edgar C. Clark, manager of the 9,600-acre Henry Ford farm, whether he could have the use of some land.

Mr. Clark smiled. The request was modest. "I guess we can spare a spot big enough for a cubic inch of seed; he said. Neither he nor the town skeptics foresaw the experiment's end.

The first year's crop gave a hint. Hayden and his aides harvested 18,000 kernels, or 50 cubic inches, which was almost three times as much as the state average.

"The first tithe," Hayden said recently, "was given to the minister of the Friends Church. He consumed it as a breakfast cereal."

The other 9/10 of the crop became the second planting. From the second harvest, 70 pounds of wheat were threshed, and a 10th of it ground into flour for cookies served at a church meeting place in Damascus, Ohio.

For a third planting, they had 63 pounds, a little more than a bushel. It was planted with high hope and it was destined to become a test of the Quaker's faith. From the start, the crop did not do well.

That winter of 1943 was hard on wheat in southern Michigan. It was cold and there was little snow for a protective blanket. Through all that part of the country, the frozen ground heaved and the damage was heavy.

Hayden watched the growing crop sadly, but by that time the late Henry Ford had become interested in the plan, and preparations were made for a gala day to mark the harvesting. A sickle had been used for the first harvest; cradles for the second; and now, for the third, Ford was lending an old Champion Self-Rake Reaper from the Edison Institute. The day dawned menacingly. Rain threatened throughout the morning, but nearly 300 persons assembled for the ceremonies.

Songs were sung, prayers were said, and Ford, pulling a New Testament from his pocket, read John 12:24, the text which had prompted Hayden to start the project. Then spry 93-year-old Harmon Russ hopped onto the old horse-drawn reaper and the work began.

It didn't begin in time. Some of the crop was bound and shocked, but a heavy afternoon rain caught most of it still lying on the ground—and this was Saturday. More rain on Sunday drenched it again and before it was finally stacked, a cloud of birds swarmed over it as if dispatched by an enemy.

In the end, that third crop produced 957 pounds of seed wheat, and from this a 10th was sold, with the proceeds, $2.67, going to the Cleveland Bible College.

For the fourth planting, this left 862 pounds, a little more than 14 bushels. It wasn't as much as Perry Hayden had hoped for, but he didn't hesitate a moment to continue the experiment.

Henry Ford let him have 14 acres, the seed was dutifully treated with Parson's Seed Saver Dust, and workmen on Ford-made tractors and John Deere drills finished the planting in an afternoon.

The fourth crop prospered. The seed was hardy. The weather was good. In midsummer, Ford, driving out to the shimmering field with Hayden, said, "I've never seen better wheat in my life."

For the harvesting, 2,500 turned out, and a day-long program brought eminent guests who included Governor Harry F. Kelly, Commissioner of Agriculture Charles Figy, Mr. and Mrs. Henry Ford and Henry Ford II.

Old-time cradlers bent their backs once more above a golden vista. Ford himself drove the ancient Self-Rake Reaper that he'd piloted as a boy. Newsreels whirred. Radio broadcasters weaved in and out. Tecumseh women moved out upon the field in a great gleaners' contest.

In midsummer, Ford, driving out to the shimmering field with Hayden, said, "I've never seen better wheat in my life."

For the threshing, there was a pageant, too. Again, a throng gathered. Ford lent historic equipment from his museum, which included a J.I. Case threshing machine originally sold to the father of Merrill C. Meigs, now vice president of the Hearst Corporation, and a Westinghouse vibrating-type thresher made in Schenectady, N.Y., in 1890.

Meigs flew in from Chicago to operate the old Case engine which ran a Case separator, and William Clark, vice president of the Case Company, went to watch the outmoded equipment still do a good day's work.

Ford mounted an old upright steam engine built by the Westinghouse Company in 1882, pulled the whistle, turned on the steam and seemed as pleased as a boy with a new toy.

Old-timers, led by David Boyd, 80, and Eugene Harris, 76, showed how wheat was threshed in biblical days, using genuine flails from the Edison Institute.

The harvest, after screening, came to 370 bushels. The tithe was sold and proceeds given to the Friends Church, and 333 bushels left for the fifth planting.

For this fifth planting, Ford planted 230 acres, a battery of his tractors drilling the field.

Again the crop did well, but Ford fell ill, and plans to hold a celebration at the field at harvesttime were canceled.

Instead of a field celebration, a token harvesting was carried out near the Friends Church, and later Ford workmen did one of the most spectacular harvesting jobs ever seen.

Forty Allis-Chalmers all-crop harvesters cut and threshed the wheat in one operation. Twelve trucks hauled the grain to bins on the Ford farm and it took two gasoline trucks, two water tanks and 67 men to keep the combines going.

The fifth-year harvest was 5,555 bushels. The tithe, $861, netted from the sale of a 10th of the crop, went to the Friends Church. That brought Hayden and his fellow townsmen into the sixth and last year of the project, and it brought them up against a problem.

Hayden and his associates had 5,000 bushels of wheat, and no land on which to plant it. One human plan after another to procure land failed, and then, Hayden said recently, "The Lord answered my prayers." Farmers from five states offered land to complete the project.

The crop was sold to them, and 276 farmers, both Protestant and Catholic, planted the 5,000 bushels, each pledging a tithe, or a 10th, of his harvest to his church.

The following summer, 1946, the final year's celebration of the experiment was planned, with Governor Kelly proclaiming Aug. 1 "Biblical Wheat Day." The fairgrounds at Adrian, Mich., was chosen as the site for the program.

Adrian businessmen, service clubs, churches and civic groups rallied to the idea.

Floats were built, the town decked with flags and bunting, and on the morning of the big day a mile-long line of cars and trucks followed the parades to the fairgrounds. At the same time, from all directions, the wheat harvest, in trucks and cars, rolled in in plump bags that were stacked by the farmers in a vast heap in front of the grandstand.

During the day, 15,000 persons packed the

grandstand and the track, applauded the entertainment features, congratulated their favorite wheat growers, and stood or sat in reverent silence during religious devotions. Two old-fashioned stone mills ground 100 pounds of wheat and a bright yellow helicopter took off with it, bound for the Lakeside Biscuit Company in Toledo, Ohio, which was to make it up in graham crackers and send them back. When the plane returned two hours later, 50 4-H girls distributed the crackers to the crowd.

The celebration ended the public's part in the six-year project. The wheat growers' accounting brought it to its official end.

The 276 farmers that year harvested 72,150 bushels, grown on 2,666 acres of land. The tithe—a 10th of the total crop—was released by the churches to the Dynamic Kernels Foundation.

William Danforth, board chairman of the Ralston Purina Company, arranged for processing the wheat into a cereal and the American Friends Service Committee distributed it overseas for famine relief. From that day, Perry Hayden carried the message for tithing up and down the country. He gave almost all his time to it, speaking in churches and civic centers. A 45-minute, color-sound film, *God Is My Landlord*, showing the steps in the wheat project from first to last, was produced and distributed. "Everywhere, people in every walk of life are accepting the tithing principle," Hayden said. "The Lord looks on tithers with favor." ❖

Henry Ford on Ford-Ferguson Model 9N tractor, 1944. Photo reprinted courtesy of the Collections of the Henry Ford Museum and Greenfield Village.

Cowboy's Prayer

O Lord, I've never lived where churches grow;
I've loved creation better as it stood
That day you finished it, so long ago,
And looked upon your work and called it good.

Just let me live my life as I've begun!
And give me work that's open to the sky;
Make me a partner of the wind and sun,
And I won't ask a life that's soft and high.

Make me as big and open as the plains;
As honest as the horse between my knees;
Clean as the wind that blows behind the rains;
Free as the hawk that circles down the breeze.

Just keep an eye on all that's done and said;
Just right me sometime when I turn aside;
And guide me on the long, dim trail ahead—
That stretches upward toward the Great Divide.

—*Author Unknown*